Super CLEAN JOKES

FOR KIDS

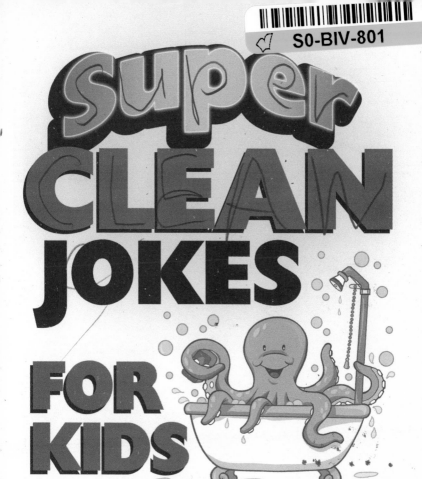

Super CLEAN JOKES FOR KIDS

BARBOUR
PUBLISHING

ISBN 978-1-60260-391-2

Published by Barbour Publishing, Inc., P.O. Box 719, Uhrichsville, Ohio 44683, www.barbourbooks.com

Our mission is to publish and distribute inspirational products offering exceptional value and biblical encouragement to the masses.

Member of the
Evangelical Christian
Publishers Association

Printed in the United States of America.

Contents

Part 2

Part 1:

ANIMALS

What do you call a puppy who loves anchovies and garlic?
A dog whose bark is a thousand times worse than his bite.

Why do skunks smell so bad?
Cheap cologne.

Why did the cow enroll in drama class?
To become a moo-vie star.

Where do space explorers leave their spacecraft?
At parking meteors.

∧∧∧∧∧∧∧∧∧∧∧∧∧∧∧∧∧∧∧∧∧∧∧∧∧∧∧∧∧

Why did the dog lie on its back with its feet sticking straight into the air?
It hoped to trip the birds.

∧∧∧∧∧∧∧∧∧∧∧∧∧∧∧∧∧∧∧∧∧∧∧∧∧∧∧∧∧

What's minty, pasty, dangerous, and kills germs?
Shark-infested toothpaste.

∧∧∧∧∧∧∧∧∧∧∧∧∧∧∧∧∧∧∧∧∧∧∧∧∧∧∧∧∧

Why did the zoo veterinarian refuse to wear a necktie?
She already had a boa-tie.

What kind of animal always is found at baseball games?
The bat.

∧∧∧∧∧∧∧∧∧∧∧∧∧∧∧∧∧∧∧∧∧∧∧∧∧∧∧∧

Why does a bear hibernate for three months
in cold weather?
We're all afraid to wake it up!

∧∧∧∧∧∧∧∧∧∧∧∧∧∧∧∧∧∧∧∧∧∧∧∧∧∧∧∧

Lorraine: "Did you know
that your dog and my
dog are brother and
sister?"
Larry: "Great! That means
we're related!"

What keys are found in the animal kingdom?
Donkeys, monkeys, and turkeys.

∧∧∧∧∧∧∧∧∧∧∧∧∧∧∧∧∧∧∧∧∧∧∧∧∧∧∧∧

How do you snatch a rug from under a polar bear?
Wait 'til the bear migrates.

∧∧∧∧∧∧∧∧∧∧∧∧∧∧∧∧∧∧∧∧∧∧∧∧∧∧∧∧

What's a lamb's favorite department store?
Woolworth's.

∧∧∧∧∧∧∧∧∧∧∧∧∧∧∧∧∧∧∧∧∧∧∧∧∧∧∧∧

What did Natasha do when she found her pet dog eating her dictionary?
She took the words right out of his mouth.

Ingrid had caught a pond turtle and kept it in captivity for a couple of days, until her parents convinced her the little animal would be much happier in the wild. Her mother was very pleased when she saw Ingrid carrying the turtle out the back door.

"Where are you taking it?" her mother asked.

"Back to the pond."

"That's wonderful, honey!"

But the next day, Ingrid's mother noticed the turtle was still around. She saw Ingrid walking out the front door with it in her palm.

"I thought you set the turtle free yesterday," her mother said.

"No, I just took it back to the pond for a visit. Today I'm taking it to the beach."

Why do moose have fur coats?
They don't like wearing cotton.

^^^^^^^^^^^^^^^^^^^^^^^^^^^^^^^^

Mike: "I heard you got kicked out of the zoo last week."

Ike: "Yeah, for feeding the squirrels."

Mike: "Wow, I know they don't like for people to feed the animals, but that seems like strong punishment."

Ike: "Actually, I was feeding the squirrels to the cougars."

^^^^^^^^^^^^^^^^^^^^^^^^^^^^^^^^

"Did you know Bobby's in the hospital?" Tracie asked.

"No, what happened?" Laurie replied.

"He went to the zoo, and the zookeeper told him the alligator would eat off his hand. So he gave it a try."

Malcolm: "Dad, when you cut down a tree, isn't it true that a new tree sometimes grows out of the stump?"

Dad: "Yes, that's been known to happen."

Malcolm: "Then if you cut off my pony's tail, will a new pony grow out of the tail?"

^^^^^^^^^^^^^^^^^^^^^^^^^^^^^^

What's black and white and furry and moves on sixteen wheels?
A skunk on skates.

^^^^^^^^^^^^^^^^^^^^^^^^^^^^^^

How do you make a skunk stop smelling?
Cut off its nose.

Martha: "I hear you've been cruel to your cat."

Jeremy: "Nonsense. I simply twirl its tail around in the air occasionally."

^^^^^^^^^^^^^^^^^^^^^^^^^^^^^^^^^

Lindsay: "Has it ever occurred to you that humans are the only animals who smoke cigarettes?"

Todd: "Well, we're the only animals who know how to strike matches."

^^^^^^^^^^^^^^^^^^^^^^^^^^^^^^^^^

Where's the best place to park dogs?
In a barking lot.

^^^^^^^^^^^^^^^^^^^^^^^^^^^^^^^^^

Why did the mouse give up tap dancing?
It kept falling in the sink.

Maria: "I can always tell when my dog is happy."
Michael: "Does he wag his tail?"
Maria: "No, but he stops biting me."

∧∧∧∧∧∧∧∧∧∧∧∧∧∧∧∧∧∧∧∧∧∧∧∧∧∧∧∧

Blake: "My dog's the smartest in town. He can say his own name in perfect English."
Alice: "What's his name?"
Blake: "Ruff."

∧∧∧∧∧∧∧∧∧∧∧∧∧∧∧∧∧∧∧∧

What do you get when you cross a polar bear and a sloth?
A giant, white, furry animal that sleeps while hanging upside-down from icicles.

Why do coyotes call at night?
The rates are cheaper.

^^^^^^^^^^^^^^^^^^^^^^^^^^^^

How do you catch a rabbit?
Hide in the bushes and sound like a carrot.

^^^^^^^^^^^^^^^^^^^^^^^^^^^^

Why did the goat stick its head through the
     barbed wire fence?
To see what was on the other side.

^^^^^^^^^^^^^^^^^^^^^^^^^^^^

Nina: "I heard you just got back from
     Africa! Did you hunt wild game?"
Stevie: "Yeah, lions."
Nina: "Did you have any luck?"
Stevie: "Yep. Didn't see a one."

What's gray and has four legs and a trunk?
a mouse on vacation.

^^^^^^^^^^^^^^^^^^^^^^^^^^^^^^^^

How do you save a hippopotamus drowning
in hot cocoa?
Throw it a marshmallow.

^^^^^^^^^^^^^^^^^^^^^^^^^^^^^^^^

What kind of dog directs traffic?
a police dog.

^^^^^^^^

How do you know if
there's a bear in
your toothpaste?
*The toothbrush is
too heavy to lift.*

What do you call a flying ape?
A hot-air baboon.

∧∧∧∧∧∧∧∧∧∧∧∧∧∧∧∧∧∧∧∧∧∧∧∧∧

oinkment: medicine for a pig with sore
    muscles.

∧∧∧∧∧∧∧∧∧∧∧∧∧∧∧∧∧∧∧∧∧∧∧∧∧

What do you do when a mouse squeaks?
Oil it.

∧∧∧∧∧∧∧∧∧∧∧∧∧∧∧∧∧∧∧∧∧∧∧∧∧

Why does the giraffe have a long neck?
So it won't have to smell its feet.

∧∧∧∧∧∧∧∧∧∧∧∧∧∧∧∧∧∧∧∧∧∧∧∧∧

Why can't you telephone the zoo?
The lion's busy.

A pet shop owner was trying to talk Mrs. McLellan into buying a dog for her children. "Oh, they'll love this little rascal!" said the clerk. "He's full of fun and he eats anything. He especially likes children."

What's black and white and has a red nose?
Rudolph the red-nosed zebra.

What was the dog doing in the mud puddle?
Making mutt pies.

Tim: "I've heard bears won't chase you at
night if you carry a flashlight."
Kim: "Depends on how fast you carry it."

∧∧∧∧∧∧∧∧∧∧∧∧∧∧∧∧∧∧∧∧∧∧∧∧∧

What do rats keep in the glove compart-
ments of their cars?
Rodent maps.

∧∧∧∧∧∧∧∧∧∧∧∧∧∧∧∧∧∧∧∧∧∧∧∧∧

What was the turtle doing on the Los
Angeles freeway?
Record time.

∧∧∧∧∧∧∧∧∧∧∧∧∧∧∧∧∧∧∧∧∧∧∧∧∧

Teacher: If I give you four hamsters and
your brother three hamsters, how many
hamsters will you have altogether?
Student: Ten. We have three already.

What's green and white and green and white and green and white?
An alligator somersaulting downhill.

^^^^^^^^^^^^^^^^^^^^^^^^^^^^^

What's the favorite city of hamsters?
Hamsterdam.

^^^^^^^^^^^^^^

What's the favorite city of chickens?
Chicago.

^^^^^^^^^^^^

Where do sheep get their hair cut?
At the baa-ber shop.

Why did the cow jump over the moon?
It forgot where it left its rocket ship.

∧∧∧∧∧∧∧∧∧∧∧∧∧∧∧∧∧∧∧∧∧∧∧∧∧∧∧

What do you call a bull taking a nap?
a bulldozer.

∧∧∧∧∧∧∧∧∧∧∧∧∧∧∧∧∧∧∧∧∧∧∧∧∧∧∧

A flock of lambs was playing in the meadow. "Baa! Baa! Baa!" they called merrily—except one lamb who insisted, "Moo! Moo! Moo!"
  "What are you saying?" they demanded.
  "I'm practicing a foreign language."

∧∧∧∧∧∧∧∧∧∧∧∧∧∧∧∧∧∧∧∧∧∧∧∧∧∧∧

Where do sheep go on vacation?
To the Baahaamaas.

Where does the farmer wash his livestock?
At the hogwash.

∧∧∧∧∧∧∧∧∧∧∧∧∧∧∧∧∧∧∧∧∧∧∧∧∧∧∧∧∧

How do you count a herd of cows?
With a cowculator.

∧∧∧∧∧∧∧∧∧∧

Where do cows go
   on dates?
To the moovies.

∧∧∧∧∧∧∧∧∧∧

Sue: "Dogs are terrible
   dancers."
Allen: "How do you
   know that?"
Sue: "They have two
   left feet."

What did Shane say when his pet snake
   crawled into the garbage disposal?
"It won't be long, now."

^^^^^^^^^^^^^^^^^^^^^^^^^^^^

Bart: "Our house was robbed last night
   while we were out."
Bret: "But I thought Butch was a great
   watchdog."
Bart: "Apparently he watched them take
   everything in sight."

^^^^^^^^^^^^^^^^^^^^^^^^^^^^

Why doesn't the cow wear a bell?
Two horns are enough warning.

^^^^^^^^^^^^^^^^^^^^^^^^^^^^

Where do injured rabbits go?
To the hopspital.

Police were investigating a break-in.
"Didn't you hear any strange noises next
   door last evening?" they asked one
   neighbor.
"We couldn't hear anything. Their dog was
   barking too loud."

∧∧∧∧∧∧∧∧∧∧∧∧∧∧∧∧∧∧∧∧∧∧∧∧∧

Why do firemen keep
   dalmatians?
*To find the fire
   hydrants.*

∧∧∧∧∧∧∧

What do you call
   a mild-mannered
   snake?
A civil serpent.

Where do all the jungle animals like to eat lunch?
At the beastro.

^^^^^^^^^^^^^^^^^^^^^^^^^^^^^^^

Teacher: "Jerry, name an animal that's a carnivore."
Jerry: "A tiger."
Teacher: "That's good. Beryl, can you name a carnivore?"
Beryl: "Another tiger."

^^^^^^^^^^^^^^^^^^^^^^^^^^^^^^^

Rachel: "Did you know dogs eat more than elephants?"
Penny: "No way! How can they do that?"
Rachel: "There are thousands of times more dogs in the world than there are elephants."

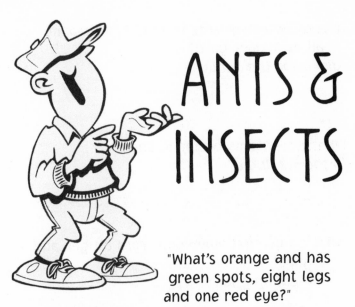

ANTS & INSECTS

"What's orange and has green spots, eight legs and one red eye?"

"I give up. What?"
"I don't know, but there's one crawling up your back."

∧∧∧∧∧∧∧∧∧∧∧∧∧∧∧∧∧∧∧∧∧∧∧∧∧∧∧∧∧

Why do spiders spin webs?
No one's ever taught them to crochet.

How do you keep ants from digging mounds
all over your yard?
Take away their shovels.

^^^^^^^^^^^^^^^^^^^^^^^^^^^^^

Where do worms prefer to shop?
In the Big Apple.

^^^^^^^^^^^^^^^^^^^^^^^^^^^^^

What do you get when you cross a tiger and
a gnat?
A man-eating gnat.

^^^^^^^^^^^^^^^^^^^^^^^^^^^^^

Teacher: "The ant is a very industrious
creature. It never seems to stop working
—and do you see what it has to show for
it?"
Student: "Yeah, it gets stepped on."

Two fleas hopped down the steps onto the sidewalk. One turned to the other and asked, "Should we walk, or take a dog?"

∧∧∧∧∧∧∧∧∧∧∧∧∧∧∧∧∧∧∧∧∧∧∧∧∧∧∧∧

Jim and Ward were camping out one summer evening, and mosquitoes were a terrible problem. About dark, a different type of insect made its presence known: fireflies, darting here and there throughout the forest.

"Wow! Look at those mosquitoes!" cried Jim.

"Oh, no!" Ward said. "I thought we could hide from them in the dark, but they're coming after us with flashlights!"

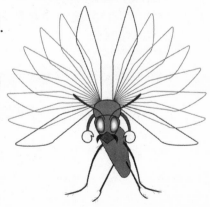

Why did the flea work overtime?
It was saving up to buy a dog.

∧∧∧∧∧∧∧∧∧∧∧∧∧∧∧∧∧∧∧∧∧∧∧∧∧∧∧∧

Why do hikers wear boots with ridged soles?
So ants will have an even chance.

∧∧∧∧∧∧∧∧∧∧∧∧∧∧∧∧∧∧∧∧∧∧∧∧∧∧∧∧

Nell: "Is it true that ants are the hardest-
   working creatures?"
Science teacher: "That's what a lot of scientists believe."
Nell: "Then why are they always attending
   picnics?"

∧∧∧∧∧∧∧∧∧∧∧∧∧∧∧∧∧∧∧∧∧∧∧∧∧∧∧∧

Did the worms enter Noah's ark in pairs?
No, in apples.

AUTOMOBILES

Eve: "Is that a pleasant highway to drive on?"
Stevie: "No, it's a cross road."

^^^^^^^^^^

Why can't car mufflers participate in marathon races?
They're too exhausted.

^^^^^^^^^^^^^^^^^^^^^^^^^^^^^^

Why did the tire get fired from its job?
It couldn't stand the pressure.

"What's wrong with your car?" a policeman asked as he approached a woman at roadside.

"I don't know. It just stopped running."

The policeman looked at the dashboard. "It's obviously out of gas," he said. "See? The needle is pointing to 'empty.'"

"Empty?" the woman said. "I thought the 'E' stood for 'enough.'"

∧∧∧∧∧∧∧∧∧∧∧∧∧∧∧∧∧∧∧∧∧∧∧∧∧∧∧∧∧

"I wish I had enough money to buy a Rolls-Royce," Jory said.

"Why do you want a Rolls-Royce?" asked Floyd.

"I don't. It's the money I want."

∧∧∧∧∧∧∧∧∧∧∧∧∧∧∧∧∧∧∧∧∧∧∧∧∧∧∧∧∧

Maria: "What would you do if you were being chased by a runaway tractor-trailer truck at seventy miles an hour?"
Karl: "Eighty."

Maggie and Sarah were driving to a party at a friend's house. The friend lived on a winding road off another winding road off another winding road in a very large neighborhood. Finally, they arrived.

"Well, I got us here," Maggie said, "but I may have to drive around awhile before I can find the right road home."

"Why can't you just put the car in reverse?" Sarah asked.

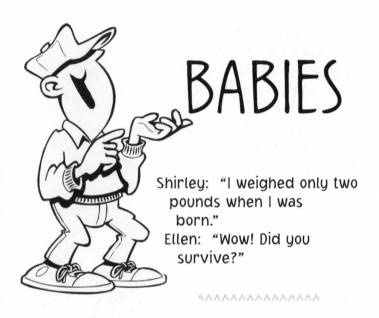

BABIES

Shirley: "I weighed only two
　　　pounds when I was
　　　born."
Ellen: "Wow! Did you
　　　survive?"

^^^^^^^^^^^^^^^^

Mother scolded her two-year-old daughter,
"Jacqueline, stop sucking your thumb."
　"Why, Mommy?" little Jacqueline asked.
　"It may be poisonous."

Kendall: "Mommy, there's a woman at the door with a baby."
Mommy: "Well, tell her we don't need any-more."

∧∧∧∧∧∧∧∧∧∧∧∧∧∧∧∧∧∧∧∧∧∧∧∧∧∧∧∧∧

Liz: "We've found a way to keep my baby brother from spilling his food all over the table."
Melinda: "How?"
Liz: "We've started feeding him on the floor."

∧∧∧∧∧∧∧∧∧∧∧∧∧∧∧∧∧∧

"What's your baby brother's name?"
"Don't know. He won't tell anybody."

BIBLE JOKES

Alice: "Grandma, were you on Noah's ark?"

Grandma: "Oh, no."

Alice: "Then how did you survive the flood?"

^^^^^^^^^^^^^^^^^^^^^^^^^^^^^^

Who was the first tennis player in the Bible?
Joseph. He served in Pharoah's court.

Sunday school teacher: "Nora, what does the Bible have to say about the Dead Sea?"

Nora: "Dead? I didn't even know it was ill!"

^^^^^^^^^^^^^^^^^^^^^^^^^^^^^^^^^^^

The Sunday school teacher asked her pupils to draw a picture of Joseph, Mary, and the Christ child fleeing from Herod. Margie drew an airplane with three faces looking out the windows.

"That's interesting," the teacher said. "Where are they going?"

"Egypt," Margie replied.

"By airplane?"

"Yes, Pontius the pilot is driving."

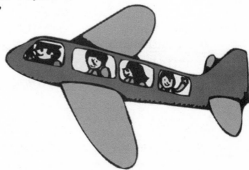

Shelby: "Do you know at what point in history God created Eve?"
Sandra: "Right after He created Adam."

∧∧∧∧∧∧∧∧∧∧∧∧∧∧∧∧∧∧∧∧∧∧∧∧∧∧

Who was most sorry when the Prodigal Son returned home?
The fatted calf.

∧∧∧∧∧∧∧∧∧∧∧∧∧∧∧∧∧∧∧∧∧∧∧∧∧∧

What kind of lights did Noah put on the ark?
Floodlights.

∧∧∧∧∧∧∧∧∧∧∧∧∧∧∧∧∧∧∧∧∧∧∧∧∧∧

What did Noah say when he'd finished loading the ark?
"Now I've herded everything."

BIRDS & BEES

What did the parrot say on
Independence Day?
Polly wanna firecracker.

^^^^^^^^^^^^^^^^^^^^^^^^^^^^^^^^

Why won't you find much honey grown in
Maryland?
There's only one B in Baltimore.

Brother: "It's a good thing you're not a swan."
Sister: "Why not?"
Brother: "You can't swim and you can't fly."

∧∧∧∧∧∧∧∧∧∧∧∧∧∧∧∧∧∧∧∧∧∧∧∧∧∧∧∧∧∧

Why do hummingbirds hum?
They've never learned the words.

∧∧∧∧∧∧∧∧∧∧∧∧∧∧∧∧∧∧∧∧∧∧∧∧∧∧∧∧∧∧

Farmer Brown and Farmer Jones were sitting in front of the country store listening to the birds in the distance.

"There's an old owl," said Farmer Brown. "Can you hear it call, 'Hoo, hoo'? "

"That's not an owl," said Farmer Jones. "It's a dove. It's saying, 'Coo, coo.' "

Farmer Brown shook his head sadly.

"I'm ashamed to say I know you. You don't recognize a 'hoo' from a 'coo.' "

What's the easiest way to imitate a bird?
Eat worms.

^^^^^^^^^^^^^^^^^^^^^^^^^^^^^^^^^

What goes "quick-quick"?
a duck with the hiccups.

^^^^^^^^^^^^^^^^^^^^^^^^^^^^^^^^^

Where do you treat an injured wasp?
at the waspital.

^^^^^^^^^^^^^^^^^^^^^^^^^^^^^^^^^

Mickie: "My bulldog came away from the
    bird show with first prize."
Vickie: "How could a
    dog do that?"
Mickie: "He ate the
    winning parrot."

Sissy: "Have you heard they're now making a special kind of ground meat out of bumblebees?"

Missy: "Yuk! What do they call that?"

Sissy: "Humburger."

^^^^^^^^^^^^^^^^^^^^^^^^^^^^^^

How do you tell a male robin from a female robin?

Call it by name. If he answers, it's a male. If she answers, it's a female.

^^^^^^^^^^^^^^^^^^^^^^^^^^^^^^

Where on Noah's ark did the bees stay?

In the ark hives.

^^^^^^^^^^^^^^^^^^^^^^^^^^^^^^

Why do owls fly around at night?

It's faster than walking.

What do you call a duck's last will and
    testament?
A legal duckument.

^^^^^^^^^^^^^^^^^^^^^^^^^^^^^^^^^

Where do ducks prefer to go on vacation?
The Duck-otas.

^^^^^^^^^^^^^^^^^^^^^^^^^^^^^^^^^

Where do wasps
    live?
Stingapore.

^^^^^^^^^

Why did Judy keep
    her pet bird in a
    fish bowl?
*The water wouldn't
    stay in a cage.*

What goes "peck-peck-peck-peck" and usually points to the north?
a magnetic woodpecker.

^^^^^^^^^^^^^^^^^^^^^^^^^^^^^

A band of pirates buried their treasure on the seashore. Afterward, they looked around for a marker but could find nothing except a few ostrich eggs. So they broke open the eggs, fried the yolks, and left the shells on top of the buried treasure.
The pirate captain announced to his crew, "Eggs mark the spot."

^^^^^^^^^^^^^^^^^^^^^^^^^^^^^

What do you get when you cross a parrot with a whippoorwill?
a bird that can sing both the words and the music.

Candice: "I'm afraid to buy eggs at the supermarket because when I break them open at home I might discover they have little chicks inside them."

Lennie: "Then why don't you buy goose eggs?"

∧∧∧∧∧∧∧∧∧∧∧∧∧∧∧∧∧∧∧∧∧∧∧∧∧∧∧∧∧

Bonnie: "Our parakeet bit my finger again this morning."

Benny: "Did you have to put anything on it?"

Bonnie: "Oh, no. He likes it plain."

∧∧∧∧∧∧∧

What do you call the Marines' pet bird?

a parrot trooper.

What do you say to a 200-pound parrot?
"Here's your box of crackers. What else would you like?"

∧∧∧∧∧∧∧∧∧∧∧∧∧∧∧∧∧∧∧∧∧∧∧∧∧∧∧∧

What kind of birds live in Central America?
Birds with suntans.

∧∧∧∧∧∧∧∧∧∧∧∧∧∧∧∧∧∧∧∧∧∧∧∧∧∧∧∧

How can you tell a guy hummingbird from a girl hummingbird?
By his mustache.

BOOKS

Little Lauren stomped up to the return desk at a department store. "Is it really true you'll give me a refund if I'm not fully satisfied with one of your products?" she asked the clerk.

"Certainly," said the clerk.

"Good," Lauren said, putting a new paperback novel on the counter. "I bought this here last week, and I don't like the ending."

Mitzy: "I just read a very stirring book."
Gordon: "What was it about?"
Mitzy: "Cooking."

^^^^^^^^^^^^^^^^^^^^^^^^^^^^^^^^

A man in a bookstore wanted to buy a book titled *How to Become a Billionaire Overnight.* But some of the pages were missing, so he complained to the shop owner.

"What's the problem?" asked the owner. "You'll still become at least a millionaire."

CHICKEN JOKES

What chicken was a famous
Antarctic explorer?
Admiral Bird.

^^^^^^^^^^^^^^^^^^^^^^^^^^^^^^^^^

Who was the least favorite president of
chickens?
*Herbert Hoover. "A chicken in every pot," he
promised.*

How do chickens stay warm?
With their central bleating system.

^^^^^^^^^^^^^^^^^^^^^^^^^^^^^^^^

Why did the chicken cross the road?
To avoid Colonel Sanders.

^^^^^^^^^^^^^^^^^^^^^^^^^^^^^^^^

Why did the chewing gum cross the road?
*It was stuck to the bottom of the chicken's
    shoe.*

^^^^^^^^^^^^^^^^^^^^^^^^^^^^^^^^

A chicken went to the doctor.
  "What's your problem?" the doctor
asked.
  "I have red, puffy spots all over my
skin."
  "Oh, no! You have the people pox!"

Why did the farmer cross the road?
To catch his chickens.

^^^^^^^^^^^^^^^^^^^^^^^^^^^^

What's the best way to move a chicken?
Pullet.

^^^^^^^^^^^^^^^^^^^^^^^^^^^^

Why did the brontosaurus
    cross the road?
*Chickens had not been
    invented.*

^^^^^^^^^^^/

"I don't like my job,"
grumbled the first
rooster.
   "Why not?" asked the
second rooster.
   "I'm working for
chicken feed."

Why do chickens have short legs?
So the eggs won't break as they're laid.

^^^^^^^^^^^^^^^^^^^^^^^^^^^^^^

Farmer: "Why aren't we having eggs for
   breakfast this morning?"
Farmer's wife: "I think the chicken mislaid
   them."

^^^^^^^^^^^^^^^^^^^^^^^^^^^^^^

What did the navy get when it crossed a
   chicken with a case of dynamite?
A mine layer.

^^^^^^^^^^^^^^^^^^^^^^^^^^^^^^

How do you catch a chicken?
*Hide in the yard and act like a corn
   kernel.*

Who is the favorite actor of chickens?
Gregory Peck.

∧∧∧∧∧∧∧∧∧∧∧∧∧∧∧∧∧∧∧∧∧∧∧∧∧∧∧∧∧∧

Why did the chicken go to New York City?
To visit the Henpire State Building.

∧∧∧∧∧∧∧∧∧∧∧∧∧∧∧∧∧∧∧∧∧∧∧∧∧∧∧∧∧∧

What is the favorite musical of chickens?
Fiddler on the Roost.

∧∧∧∧∧∧∧∧∧∧

How does a chicken
    farmer wake up
    in the morning?
*Probably with an alarm
    clock.*

Why did the rooster cluck at midnight?
His cluck was fast.

∧∧∧∧∧∧∧∧∧∧∧∧∧∧∧∧∧∧∧∧∧∧∧∧∧∧∧

Why did the rock band hire a chicken?
They needed the drumsticks.

∧∧∧∧∧∧∧∧∧∧∧∧∧∧∧∧∧∧∧∧∧∧∧∧∧∧

Why was the chicken sitting on the egg-
    plant?
She was nearsighted.

CLOTHES

"Lane, look at you!" shrieked his mother. "You've ruined your brand-new suit falling into the mud!"

"I'm sorry," Lane said. "I didn't have time to take it off before I hit the water."

^^^^^^^^^^^^^^^^^^^^^^^^^^^^^^^^^^^^

Sherie: "Mommy, can I try on that dress in the window?"
Mother: "No, you'll have to go to the dressing room."

Why did Christy put on a wet dress?
Because the label said "Wash and Wear."

^^^^^^^^^^^^^^^^^^^^^^^^^^^^^

Missy: "I just got a new pair of alligator shoes!"
Sissy: "I didn't know you had an alligator."

^^^^^^^^^^^^^^^^^^^^^^^^^^^^^

Wren: "Don't you realize your umbrella has a hole in it?"
Adrienne: "Sure. It lets me check and see when the rain stops."

^^^^^^^^^^^^^^^^^^^^^^^^^^^^^

Polly: "Why are you wearing all those clothes to go paint the fence?"
Agnes: "The can says you need two coats to do a good job."

CRAZY FOLKS

Why did the woman remove her nose?
To see what made it run.

^^^^^^^^^^^^^^^^^^^^^^^^^^^^^^

Why did the carpenter put his finger over
the head of the nail he was hammering?
To muffle the noise.

Warren: "Lester sure has a weird sense of humor."

Katrina: "How so?"

Warren: "We went into an antique shop yesterday, and he asked the owner, 'What's new?' "

∧∧∧∧∧∧∧∧∧∧∧∧∧∧∧∧∧∧∧∧∧∧∧∧∧∧∧∧∧∧

"Veronica has got to be the nicest person ever born," said Andrew.

"What makes you think so?" asked Arthur.

"She says 'thank you' to automatic sliding doors."

∧∧∧∧∧∧∧∧∧∧∧∧∧∧∧∧∧∧∧∧∧∧∧∧∧∧∧∧∧∧

Dennis: "Steve's changed his mind again."

Suzanne: "Well, I hope this one's got more sense than the last one he had."

Susan: "We have a terrible problem. Our
mother thinks she's a chicken."
Wanda: "Why don't you take her to a psychiatrist?"
Susan: "We need the eggs."

^^^^^^^^^^^^^^^^^^^^^^^^^^^^^^^

Ray: "It's dark in here. Strike a match."
Roy: "I'm trying to, but this match won't
light."
Ray: "Is it wet?"
Roy: "I don't think so. It
worked a minute ago."

^^^^^^^^^^^

Wilt: "You have a
stately nose, sir."
Mort: "Why thank you.
I picked it myself."

Michael: "Why are you making faces at my dog? That's silly."

Artie: "Well, he started it."

^^^^^^^^^^^^^^^^^^^^^^^^^^^^^

Melissa: "I think Cathy's a little distracted. She sure is wasting a lot of money."

Sandi: "Oh? How?"

Melissa: "Well, for example, she's been going to a lot of drive-in movies lately."

Sandi: "That sounds pretty normal to me—and cheap."

Melissa: "But she takes a taxi."

^^^^^^^^^^^^^^^^^^^^^^^^^^^^^

"My son thinks he's a dog. He barks at people and chases cars and cats."

"How long has he behaved this way?"

"Basically, since he was a puppy."

DEFINITIONS

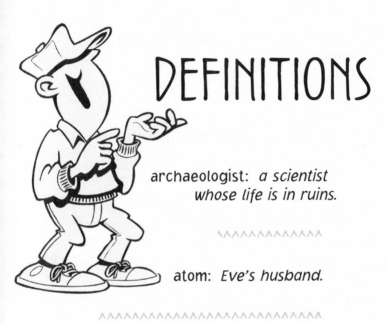

archaeologist: *a scientist whose life is in ruins.*

^^^^^^^^^^^^

atom: *Eve's husband.*

^^^^^^^^^^^^^^^^^^^^^^^^^^^

autobiography: *a book about a car.*

^^^^^^^^^^^^^^^^^^^^^^^^^^

bookkeeper: *a person who doesn't return library books on time.*

bowling balls: *what elephants use for marbles.*

^^^^^^^^^^^^^^^^^^^^^^^^^^^^

cartoon: *a song about an automobile.*

^^^^^^^^^^^^^^^^^^^^^^^^^^^^

cashew: *the way nuts sneeze.*

^^^^^^^^^^^^^^^^^^^^^^^^^^^^

catsup: *what you have to do when you're behind.*

^^^^^^^^^^^^^^^^^^^^^^^^^^^^

Cheerios: *what tiny people use for life preservers.*

Cheerios: *donut seeds.*

∧∧∧∧∧∧∧∧∧∧∧∧∧∧∧∧∧∧∧∧∧∧∧∧∧∧∧

chipmunk: *a monkey eating potato chips.*

∧∧∧∧∧∧∧∧∧∧∧∧∧∧∧∧∧∧∧∧∧∧∧∧∧∧∧

circle: *a line that meets its other end in secret.*

∧∧∧∧∧∧∧∧∧∧∧∧∧∧∧∧∧∧∧∧∧∧∧∧∧∧∧

commentator: *an everyday potato.*

∧∧∧∧∧

coquette: *a small cola.*

dentist's office: *a filling station.*

∧∧∧∧∧∧∧∧∧∧∧∧∧∧∧∧∧∧∧∧∧∧∧∧∧∧∧

disease: *de seven big bodies of water where de ships sail.*

∧∧∧∧∧∧∧∧∧∧∧∧∧∧∧∧∧∧∧∧∧∧∧∧∧∧∧

dogwood: *the tree with the loudest bark.*

∧∧∧∧∧∧∧∧∧∧∧∧∧∧∧∧∧∧∧∧∧∧∧∧∧∧∧

don't: *short for "doughnut."*

∧∧∧∧∧∧∧∧∧∧∧∧∧∧∧∧∧∧∧∧∧∧∧∧∧∧∧

drydock: *a thirsty surgeon.*

∧∧∧∧∧∧∧∧∧∧∧∧∧∧∧∧∧∧∧∧∧∧∧∧∧∧∧

enormous: *a very large moose.*

footnote: *a sound you play with your feet.*

^^^^^^^^^^^^^^^^^^^^^^^^^^^^^

frozen police officers: *copsicles.*

^^^^^^^^^^^^^^^^^^^^^^^^^^^^

hippie: *what holds up your leggie.*

^^^^^^^^^^^^^^^^^^^^^^^^^^^^

horse doctor: *a doctor with a sore throat.*

^^^^^^^

humbug: *a roach who loves music.*

lambchops: *the way sheep cut their firewood.*

∧∧∧∧∧∧∧∧∧∧∧∧∧∧∧∧∧∧∧∧∧∧∧∧∧∧∧∧

lemonade: *helping a lemon cross the street.*

∧∧∧∧∧∧∧∧∧∧∧∧∧∧∧∧∧∧∧∧∧∧∧∧∧∧∧∧

mischief: *the police chief's wife.*

∧∧∧∧∧∧∧∧∧∧∧∧∧∧∧∧∧∧∧∧∧∧∧∧∧∧∧∧

mountain range: *a cookstove inside a cabin in the Rockies.*

∧∧∧∧∧∧∧∧∧∧∧∧∧∧∧∧∧∧∧∧∧∧∧∧∧∧∧∧

mushroom: *the room where Eskimos train their sled dogs.*

panther: *a person who manufactures panths.*

∧∧∧∧∧∧∧∧∧∧∧∧∧∧∧∧∧∧∧∧∧∧∧∧∧∧∧

pineapple: *the fruit of a pine tree.*

∧∧∧∧∧∧∧∧∧

pocket calculator: *a device for counting pockets.*

∧∧∧∧∧∧∧∧∧∧∧∧∧

polygon: *a deceased parrot.*

∧∧∧∧∧∧∧∧∧∧∧∧∧∧∧∧∧∧

raisin: *a worried grape.*

short-order cook: *a person who prepares food for children.*

∧∧∧∧∧∧∧∧∧∧∧∧∧∧∧∧∧∧∧∧∧∧∧∧∧∧∧∧

stagecoach: *a theatrical instructor.*

∧∧∧∧∧∧∧∧∧∧∧∧∧∧∧∧∧∧∧∧∧∧∧∧∧∧∧∧

stucco: *what happens when you step on a piece of used bubble gummo.*

∧∧∧∧∧∧∧∧∧∧∧∧∧∧∧∧∧∧∧∧∧∧∧∧∧∧∧∧

Sugar Bowl: *where flies play championship football.*

∧∧∧∧∧∧∧∧∧∧∧∧∧∧∧∧∧∧∧∧∧∧∧∧∧∧∧∧

Super Bowl: *swimming pool for Superman's goldfish.*

teacher's pet: *student of a teacher who can't afford a cat.*

^^^^^^^^^^^^^^^^^^^^^^^^^^^^^

thumbtacks: *a tax on thumbs.*

^^^^^^^^^^^^^^^^^^^^^^^^^^^^^

toadstool: *a place for a frog to sit down.*

^^^^^^^^^^^^^^^^^^^^^^^^^^^^^

unaware: *what you put on first and take off last.*

^^^^^^^^^^^

watershed: *a haven for ships in the middle of the ocean.*

venison: *a type of meat that costs deerly.*

∧∧∧∧∧∧∧∧∧∧∧∧∧∧∧∧∧∧∧∧∧∧∧∧∧∧∧∧

vipers: *the things that keep car vindows clear venever it rains.*

∧∧∧∧∧∧∧∧∧∧∧∧∧∧∧∧∧∧∧∧∧∧∧∧∧∧∧∧

waterbed: *where fish sleep.*

∧∧∧∧∧∧∧∧∧∧∧∧∧∧∧∧∧∧∧∧∧∧∧∧∧∧∧∧

zebra: *a horse in prison.*

∧∧∧∧∧∧∧∧∧∧∧∧∧∧∧∧∧∧∧∧∧∧∧∧∧∧∧∧

zinc: *what happens to you in the water if you can't zwim.*

DOCTORS

What do you call a surgeon with eight arms?
a doctopus.

∧∧∧∧∧∧∧∧∧∧∧

Patient: "Doc, can you make house calls?"
Doctor: "That depends. How sick is the house?"

∧∧∧∧∧∧∧∧∧∧∧∧∧∧∧∧∧∧∧∧∧∧∧∧∧∧∧∧∧

What kind of people enjoy bad health?
Doctors.

What did the doctor say to the woman who
 swallowed a spoon?
"Sit still and don't stir."

∧∧∧∧∧∧∧∧∧∧∧∧∧∧∧∧∧∧∧∧∧∧∧∧∧∧∧∧

Doctor: "I want you to drink plenty of
 liquids so you'll get over this cold."
Mrs. Martin: "I never drink anything else."

∧∧∧∧∧∧∧∧∧∧∧∧∧∧∧∧∧∧∧∧∧∧∧∧∧∧∧∧

What do you call a bone specialist from
 Egypt?
A Cairopractor.

∧∧∧∧∧∧∧∧∧∧∧∧∧∧∧∧∧∧∧∧∧∧∧∧∧∧∧∧

Eye doctor: "You need a new pair of glasses."
Patient: "How do you know that? You
 haven't examined me yet."
Doctor: "Because you just came in through
 my office window."

How is a surgeon like a comedian?
They both keep you in stitches.

^^^^^^^^^^^^^^^^^^^^^^^^^^^^^^^^^

A woman barged into a doctor's office and demanded attention.
"I dreamed I ate a giant marshmallow!" she screamed.

"Control yourself," said the reception- ist. "It was only a dream."

"No dream! When I woke up, my pillow was missing!"

Woman: "My husband snores so loudly he keeps everybody in the house awake. What can we do?"

Doctor: "Try turning him on his side, massaging his shoulders and neck, and stuffing a washcloth into his mouth."

∧∧∧∧∧∧∧∧∧∧∧∧∧∧∧∧∧∧∧∧∧∧∧∧∧∧∧

What do you call foot X-rays?
Footographs.

ELEPHANTS

Why are elephants so wrinkled?
They stay in the bathtub too long.

^^^^^^^^^^^

Why are elephants so wrinkled?
They're too difficult to iron.

^^^^^^^^^^^^^^^^^^^^^^^^^^^^

How do elephants communicate?
With elephones.

How do you make an elephant float?
Start with your favorite ice cream, pour cola over it, and add elephant.

∧∧∧∧∧∧∧∧∧∧∧∧∧∧∧∧∧∧∧∧∧∧∧∧∧∧∧∧

Why is a snail small and smooth?
Because if it were huge and wrinkled, it would be an elephant.

∧∧∧∧∧∧∧∧∧∧∧∧∧∧∧∧∧∧∧∧∧∧∧∧∧∧∧∧

What's big and gray and has a trunk and goes "zrrrrrrrrrrrr"?
An outboard elephant.

∧∧∧∧∧∧∧∧∧∧∧∧∧∧∧∧∧∧∧∧∧∧∧∧∧∧∧∧

What's the difference between Superman and an elephant?
The elephant wears a big "E" on his chest.

Why was the elephant wearing a purple T-shirt?
His other shirts were all at the cleaners.

∧∧∧∧∧∧∧∧∧∧∧∧∧∧∧∧∧∧∧∧∧∧∧∧∧∧∧∧∧

How do you treat an elephant with sea-sickness?
Give it a lot of space.

∧∧∧∧∧∧∧∧∧∧∧∧∧∧∧∧∧∧∧∧∧∧∧∧∧∧∧∧∧

Why are elephants gray?
So you can tell them apart from bananas.

What's the best way to tell a kitten from an elephant?
Try picking it up. If it's too heavy, it's surely an elephant.

∧∧∧∧∧∧∧∧∧∧∧∧∧∧∧∧∧∧∧∧∧∧∧∧∧∧∧∧∧

What's the difference between an elephant in Africa and an elephant in India?
Several thousand miles.

FARM JOKES

One rooster said to another, "You don't want to mess with the new rooster in the yard. He's mean."

"How do you know?" asked the second rooster.

"He came from a hard-boiled egg."

∧∧∧∧∧∧∧∧∧∧∧∧∧∧∧∧∧∧∧∧∧∧∧∧∧∧∧∧

What did the farmer say to the sheep?
"Hey, ewe!"

Mary was visiting her grandparents on the farm. "That little pig sure eats a lot of corn," she said.

"He has to make a hog of himself," said Grandmother, "or he'll never be full-grown."

∧∧∧∧∧∧∧∧∧∧∧∧∧∧∧∧∧∧∧∧∧∧∧∧∧∧∧∧∧

Why did the farmer put razor blades in the potato patch?
He wanted to grow potato chips.

∧∧∧∧∧∧∧∧∧∧∧∧∧∧∧∧∧∧∧∧∧∧∧∧∧∧∧∧∧

Farmer: "You know, the people in my little town are smarter than the people in your big city."
City feller: "How do you get that?"
Farmer: "We know where L.A. is, but you don't know where Podunk is."

Why did the farmer spend the day stomping
   his field?
He wanted mashed potatoes.

^^^^^^^^^^^^^^^^^^^^^^^^^

What did the farmer say to the ?
"I'm very sorry but I have to mow now.

^^^^^^^^^^^^

What did the farmer
   do at the choco-
   late factory?
Milk chocolates.

^^^^^^^^^^

What did the pea
   patch say to the
   corn patch?
Stop stalking me.

First farmer: "Did the tornado damage your barn last night?"

Second farmer: "I don't know. Haven't found it yet."

^^^^^^^^^^^^^^^^^^^^^^^^^^^^^^

Elaine: "My uncle just bought a farm that's a mile long and an inch wide.

Penny: "What does he think he can grow on land like that?"

Elaine: "Spaghetti, I guess."

^^^^^^^^^^^^^^^^^^^^^^^^^^^^^^

Betsy and Pat were roaming the meadows of their grandparents' farm when they encountered a dangerous-looking bull.

"Are you afraid?" asked Pat.

"Not me," said Betsy. "I'm a vegetarian."

Why did the farmer raise his children in a barn?
He wanted them to grow up in a stable environment.

∧∧∧∧∧∧∧∧∧∧∧∧∧∧∧∧∧∧∧∧∧∧∧∧∧∧∧∧∧∧∧

When do you hear the shout, "Ready. . . Set. . .Hoe"?
At the beginning of a race between two farmers.

∧∧∧∧∧∧

Robby: "What would you do if a bull charged?"

Toby: "I'd give him all the time he wanted to pay off the bill."

FOOD

Muldrow: "When did Caesar utter the famous statement, 'Et tu, Brute?'"

Muldoon: "When Brutus asked him how many cheeseburgers he'd had at the cookout."

∧∧∧∧∧∧∧∧∧∧∧∧∧∧∧∧∧∧∧∧∧∧∧∧∧∧∧∧∧

Coreen: "I ate a yo-yo lunch."

Sonny: "What's a yo-yo lunch?"

Coreen: "Soon after you get it down, it comes up again."

What did one hot dog say to the other?
"Frankly, I prefer cheeseburgers."

^^^^^^^^^^^^^^^^^^^^^^^^^^^^^^^

What's the difference between a jar of
peanut butter and a freight train?
*A freight train doesn't stick to the
roof of your mouth.*

^^^^^^^^^^^^^^^^^^^^

How do you deliver fried pies to
customers?
On piecycles.

^^^^^^^^^^^^^

Why was Miss Muffet
reading a map?
Because she'd lost her whey.

What's the favorite food of Martians?
Martianmallows.

∧∧∧∧∧∧∧∧∧∧∧∧∧∧∧∧∧∧∧∧∧∧∧∧∧∧∧

What's the difference between an Oreo
    cookie and a cheeseburger?
Oreos taste much better dunked in milk.

∧∧∧∧∧∧∧∧∧∧∧∧∧∧∧∧∧∧∧∧∧∧∧∧∧∧∧

One Irish potato said to the other Irish
potato, "I'm about to change my
nationality."
    "How are you going to do that?"
    "By becoming French fries."

∧∧∧∧∧∧∧∧∧∧∧∧∧∧∧∧∧∧∧∧∧∧∧∧∧∧∧

Ingrid: "Do you know what makes the Tower
    of Pisa lean?"
Peter: "It's malnourished, I guess."

How do you tell a chili pepper from a bell pepper?
The chili pepper always wears a jacket.

∧∧∧∧∧∧∧∧∧∧∧∧∧∧∧∧∧∧∧∧∧∧∧∧∧∧∧∧∧

What did one cannibal say to the other as they gobbled up a clown?
"This food tastes funny."

∧∧∧∧∧∧∧∧∧∧∧∧∧

What's the favorite lunch item in Iceland?
Chili dogs.

∧∧∧∧∧∧∧∧∧

What happened when Grandma served ostrich instead of turkey for Thanksgiving dinner?
It buried its head in the pumpkin pie.

Father: "It's proper manners to eat your
food with your fork, not your spoon."
Marvin: "But my fork leaks."

∧∧∧∧∧∧∧∧∧∧∧∧∧∧∧∧∧∧∧∧∧∧∧∧∧∧∧∧∧

A prospector straggled into town, went
into the little cafe and told the owner,
"Buddy, I'm starved almost to death.
It's been two weeks since I've tasted food."
  The bartender responded, "Well, it all
tastes about the same as it did back
then."

∧∧∧∧∧∧∧∧∧∧∧∧∧∧∧∧∧∧∧∧∧∧∧∧∧∧∧∧∧

Chris: "I have to eat very balanced
meals."
Burt: "I didn't know you were so health-
conscious."
Chris: "I'm not, really. I'm training to be a
tightrope walker."

Thomas: "Gerald sure does love Chinese food."

Veronica: "Yeah, I think he's a chow meiniac."

∧∧∧∧∧∧∧∧∧∧∧∧∧∧∧∧∧∧∧∧∧∧∧∧∧∧∧∧∧

Rene: "How do you like those crab apples?"

Richard: "They taste rather salty, for apples."

∧∧∧∧∧∧∧∧∧∧∧

What did the gingerbread man do when his eyesight failed?
Bought contact chocolate chips.

Teacher: "Marvin, you haven't washed. I can see food on your face."

Marvin: "What food?"

Teacher: "The eggs you had for breakfast this morning."

Marvin: "Eggs? I had cereal for breakfast this morning. The eggs must be from yesterday morning."

∧∧∧∧∧∧∧∧∧∧∧∧∧∧∧∧∧∧∧∧∧∧∧∧∧∧∧∧∧∧

What did the butcher get when he crossed a chicken with King Kong?

a giant drumstick.

∧∧∧∧∧∧∧∧∧∧∧∧∧∧∧∧∧∧∧∧∧∧∧∧∧∧∧∧∧∧

Why did the tangerine go to the movies alone?

It couldn't find a date.

Maria: "You can have my M&Ms."
Alex: "You don't like candy?"
Maria: "Not this kind. Too hard to peel."

How can you tell if a rattlesnake has been
  drinking your
  milk?
*By the two fang
  marks in the
  carton.*

What do you get if you
  cross a bulldog with
  a bull?
*A burger that can bite
  back.*

FROGS

What goes "CROAK! CROAK!"
on foggy nights?
a froghorn.

^^^^^^^^^^^^

What's green and stands
in a corner?
a frog that got caught talking in class.

^^^^^^^^^^^^^^^^^^^^^^^^^^^^^^

What's white on the outside, green on the
inside, and makes croaking sounds?
a frog sandwich.

GROWN-UPS

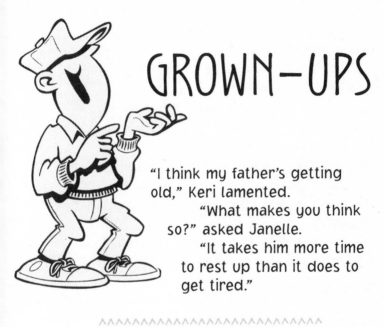

"I think my father's getting old," Keri lamented.

"What makes you think so?" asked Janelle.

"It takes him more time to rest up than it does to get tired."

^^^^^^^^^^^^^^^^^^^^^^^^^^^^^^^^

Sally: "My mother has trained herself to walk in her sleep every night."

Cal: "Why would she want to do that?"

Sally: "To save time. This way she can get her exercise and her rest all at once."

"Grandpa, why don't you ever read the newspaper?"

"I don't want to put any needless wear on my spectacles."

^^^^^^^^^^^^^^^^^^^^^^^^^^^^^^^

Grandma was giving Sarah some wise advice: "Never put off until tomorrow what you can do today. Do you understand what I mean?"

"Yes, Grandma. It means we should finish this apple pie right now."

^^^^^^^^^^^^^^^^^^^^^^^^^^^^^^^

"I don't think my mom is a very smart parent," Jill said.

"Why not?" asked Grace Ann.

"She's always sending me to bed when I'm not sleepy and making me get up when I'm still tired."

Patti: "How do you do today?"
Grumpy Grandpa: "How do I do what?"

∧∧∧∧∧∧∧∧∧∧∧∧∧∧∧∧∧∧∧∧∧∧∧∧∧∧∧∧∧∧

Kendra: "Martin, what will you do when you
    grow up to be as big as your daddy?"
Martin: "Go on a diet, first of all."

∧∧∧∧∧∧∧∧∧∧

Don: "My parents
    once crossed
    the Atlantic with
    Elizabeth on the
    Queen Elizabeth II."
Dean: "You mean
    they got to
    know the
    queen?"
Don: "No, they
    were with my
    grandmother
    Elizabeth."

Some grown-ups are as hard to wake up as sleeping bags.

^^^^^^^^^^^^^^^^^^^^^^^^^^^^^^^

Bailey: "Why does your dad wrap newspapers all over himself?"
Barry: "He likes to dress with *The Times*."

^^^^^^^^^^^^^^^^^^^^^^^^^^^^^^^

Why did Mommy tip-toe past the medicine cabinet?
She didn't want to wake up the sleeping pills.

^^^^^^^^^^^^^^^^^^^^^^^^^^^^^^^

Mother: "Stan, wash your face."
Stan: "It's not fair."
Mother: "What do you mean?"
Stan: "Dad has less to wash because of his beard."

"I figured out how to make my dad laugh on Sunday."

"Really? How?"

"I told him a joke on Friday."

^^^^^^^^^^^^^^^^^^^^^^^^^^^^^^

Mother: "Troy, I've been calling you for the last five minutes! Didn't you hear me?"

Troy: "No, I didn't hear you until the fourth time you called."

^^^^^^^^^^^^^^^

David: "My dad never gets his hair wet when he showers."

Nan: "Does he wear a shower cap?"

David: "Nope. He's bald."

"Mom, may I go upstairs and play with the guinea pig?" Daniel asked.

"Why son, why would you want to see a guinea pig when Grandmom is here visiting?"

∧∧∧∧∧∧∧∧∧∧∧∧∧∧∧∧∧∧∧∧∧∧∧∧∧∧∧∧∧∧

"My grandmother is always complaining about how awful it feels to be old," Carmen said.

"Mine, too," said Dixie. "I guess those wrinkles hurt a lot."

∧∧∧∧∧∧∧∧∧∧∧∧∧∧∧∧∧∧∧∧∧∧∧∧∧∧∧∧∧∧

Sal: "I can't think of a good present for Mom on Mother's Day."
Val: "Why not lipstick?"
Sal: "Nah. . .I'm not sure what size her mouth is."

"Do you get spanked much?" a child asked his friend.

"Yes. I think I'm the kind of boy my parents don't want me to play with."

^^^^^^^^^^^^^^^^^^^^^^^^^^^^^^^

Rachel: "Do you know the difference between Daddy's toys and our brother's toys?"
Fran: "Yeah, Daddy's cost a lot more money."

^^^^^^^^^^^

Earl: "Wanna know a funny coincidence about my parents?"
Virl: "Sure. What?"
Earl: "They were both married at the same time, same day, same year—and same place!"

HISTORY

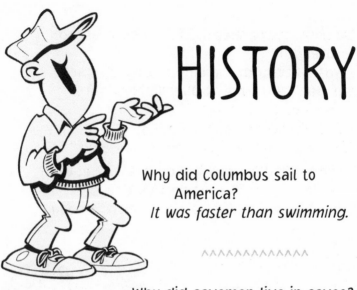

Why did Columbus sail to America?
It was faster than swimming.

ΛΛΛΛΛΛΛΛΛΛΛΛΛ

Why did cavemen live in caves?
They couldn't afford condominiums.

ΛΛΛΛΛΛΛΛΛΛΛΛΛΛΛΛΛΛΛΛΛΛΛΛΛΛ

Why did the Romans build straight roads?
So their enemies couldn't hide around the curves.

Teacher: "How long did the Hundred Years' War last?"

Student: "I don't know. Ten years?"

Teacher: "No! Think carefully. How old is a five-year-old horse?"

Student, thoughtfully: "Oh, five years old!"

Teacher: "That's right. So how long did the Hundred Years' War last?"

Student: "Now I get it—five years!"

∧∧∧∧∧∧∧∧∧∧∧∧

The teacher held up a picture of Abraham Lincoln and asked the class, "Can anyone tell me who this is?"

"I know!" shouted Mindy. "He's the man who owns all the pennies."

History teacher: "What English monarch was also an amateur doctor?"
Jamie: "William the Corn Curer?"

∧∧∧∧∧∧∧∧∧∧∧∧∧∧∧∧∧∧∧∧∧∧∧∧∧∧

Teacher: "What was the Romans' most famous achievement?"
Pupil: "They could read Latin."

∧∧∧∧∧∧∧∧∧∧∧∧∧∧∧∧∧∧∧∧∧∧∧∧∧∧

History teacher: "Now Wally, what can you tell us about President Millard Fillmore?"
Wally: "He's dead."

∧∧∧∧∧∧∧∧∧∧∧∧∧∧∧∧∧∧∧∧∧∧∧∧∧∧

Baker: "I wish I'd been born about four thousand years ago."
Brewster: "Why?"
Baker: "So I wouldn't have to learn so much history."

How did the ancient Vikings communicate?
Norse Code.

^^^^^^^^^^^^^^^^^^^^^^^^^^^^^^^^^^

A history teacher was discussing the early American explorers. "Merrivale the Monk spent years living with the native Americans, learning their songs," she said. "The Indians gave him a special name. Do you know what it was, Jack?"

"Tone-Deaf," guessed Jack.

^^^^^^^^^^^^^

Where did Lincoln sign the Emancipation Proclamation?
At the bottom of the last page.

Teacher: "Who won at Bull Run?"
Student: "Was that a tennis match or a horse race?"

∧∧∧∧∧∧∧∧∧∧∧∧∧∧∧∧∧∧∧∧∧∧∧∧∧∧∧∧∧∧

Lana: "My great-great-great-grandparents were the first citizens of this town."
Kurt: "That's nothing. My ancestors fought in the Revolutionary War."
Lana: "My ancestors fought in ancient Rome."
Kurt: "My ancestors fought for Alexander the Great before that."
Lana: "My ancestors were on the ark with Noah."
Kurt: "My ancestors had their own ship."

∧∧∧∧∧∧∧∧∧∧∧∧∧∧∧∧∧∧∧∧∧∧∧∧∧∧∧∧∧∧

What do history teachers talk about when they get together?
The old days.

William: "Did you hear the North and South are going to refight the Battle of Kennesaw Mountain?"
Wade: "What for?"
William: "Because it wasn't fought on the level the first time."

∧∧∧∧∧∧∧∧∧∧∧∧∧∧∧∧∧∧∧∧∧∧∧∧∧∧∧∧∧∧∧

Teacher: "What do you think George Washington would say about America if he were alive today?"
Student: "Doesn't matter. He would be so old, his ideas would be completely useless."

HOUSES

Two carpenters were building a house. One examined every nail before using it and ended up throwing half of them away.

"Why are you wasting those nails?" his partner asked.

"They're no good. The sharp points are on the wrong end."

"Yeah, but you could use those for the other side of the house.

Marcia: "How do you like your new house?"
Kyle: "It's okay, but kinda small. We had to remove the paint from the walls in order to make all our furniture fit."

∧∧∧∧∧∧∧∧∧∧∧∧∧∧∧∧∧∧∧∧∧∧∧∧∧∧∧∧∧

Dee Dee: "Did you know Santa Claus has a secret fear of crawling down chimneys?"

Pee Wee: "No! Is he afraid of closed-in places?"

Dee Dee: "Yes. It's called Claustrophobia."

KITCHEN JOKES

Ginger: "Mommy, I need another glass of milk."

Mommy: "You've had two already. Why are you so thirsty this morning?"

Ginger: "I'm not. I'm checking to see if my throat leaks."

^^^^^^^^^^^^^^^^^^^^^^^^^^^^^^^

How do goblins order their eggs?
Horrifried.

Mother: "Joy, haven't you finished making the Kool-Aid yet?"
Joy: "I'm having trouble getting the water into the envelope."

∧∧∧∧∧∧∧∧∧∧∧∧∧∧∧∧∧∧∧∧∧∧∧∧∧∧∧∧∧∧

Where do hot dogs dance?
At meatballs.

∧∧∧∧∧∧∧∧∧∧∧∧∧∧∧∧∧∧∧

What are the four seasons?
Salt, pepper, catsup, and mayonnaise.

∧∧∧∧∧∧∧∧∧∧∧∧∧∧∧∧∧∧

How can you tell if there's a horse in your refrigerator?
By the hoofprints in the butter.

Beth: "Would you like to join me in a cup of
　　tea?"
Veronica: "I don't think we'd both fit."

^^^^^^^^^^^^^^^^^^^^^^^^^^^^^

Liz: "My mom's not a very good cook."
Trish: "Does breakfast taste awful?"
Liz: "No, just weird. She can't even get
　　a Pop-Tart out of the toaster in one
　　piece."

^^^^^^^^^^^^^^^^^^^^^^^^^^^^^

How do you repair a broken casserole dish?
With tomato paste.

^^^^^^^^^^^^^^^^^^^^^^^^^^^^^

What did Mary have for supper?
A little lamb.

Paul: "Why are you staring at that frozen orange juice can?"

Donna: "Can't you see? It says 'concentrate.' "

∧∧∧∧∧∧∧∧∧∧∧∧∧∧∧∧∧∧∧∧∧∧∧∧∧∧∧∧∧∧∧∧

Mom, entering the kitchen: "I see you've been making chocolate chip cookies."

Marsha: "Can you smell them in the oven already?"

Mom: "No, but I notice M&M shells all over the floor."

∧∧∧∧∧∧∧∧∧∧∧∧∧∧∧∧∧

What ice cream dessert is brown, white, and red?
a chocolate sundae with catsup.

KNOCK-KNOCK JOKES

Knock-knock.
Who's there?
Howie.
Howie Who?
Howie gonna win the baseball game if you won't come out and play?

Knock-knock.
Who's there?
Butcher.
Butcher Who?
Butcher hands up! This is a robbery!

^^^^^^^^^^^^^^^^^^^^^^^^^^^^

Knock-knock.
Who's there?
Abbey.
Abbey Who?
Abbey birthday to
you. . . .

^^^^^^^^

Knock-knock.
Who's there?
Howard.
Howard Who?
Howard is it to lift a
piano?

Knock-knock.
Who's there?
Dune.
Dune Who?
Dune anything in particular this afternoon?

^^^^^^^^^^^^^^^^^^^^^^^^^^^^^^^^

Knock-knock.
Who's there?
Pasta.
Pasta Who?
Pasta gravy, please.

^^^^^^^^^^^^^^^^^^^^^^^^^^^^^^^^

Knock-knock.
Who's there?
Luke.
Luke Who?
Luke at me twirl my hula hoop!

Knock-knock.
   Who's there?
Irish.
   Irish Who?
Irish you would open the door.

^^^^^^^^^^^^^^^^^^^^^^^^^^^^^^^

Knock-knock.
   Who's there?
Peas.
   Peas Who?
Peas open the door and let me in.

^^^^^^^^^^^^

Knock-knock.
   Who's there?
Snakeskin.
   Snakeskin Who?
Snakeskin hurtchew, if
you ain't keerful.

Knock-knock.
  Who's there?
Fanny.
  Fanny Who?
Fannybody wants to come out and play, I'm waiting.

^^^^^^^^^^^^^^^^^^^^^^^^^^^^^^^^

Knock-knock.
  Who's there?
Tock.
  Tock Who?
Tock to me. I'm lonely.

^^^^^^^^^^^^^^^^^^^^^^^^^^^^^^^^

Knock-knock.
  Who's there?
Cinnamon.
  Cinnamon Who?
Cinnamon dressed in blue pass by here lately?

Knock-knock.
Who's there?
Staten Island.
Staten Island Who?
Staten Island I see out there in the water?

∧∧∧∧∧∧∧∧∧∧∧∧∧∧∧∧∧∧∧∧∧∧∧∧∧∧∧∧∧

Knock-knock.
Who's there?
Midas.
Midas Who?
Midas well let me in. I'm not
going anywhere.

∧∧∧∧∧∧∧∧∧

Knock-knock.
Who's there?
Arthur.
Arthur Who?
Arthur any mean
dogs around here?

Knock-knock.

Who's there?

Phillip.

Phillip Who?

Phillip the dog's water bowl, please. He's very thirsty.

^^^^^^^^^^^^^^^^^^^^^^^^^^^^^^

Knock-knock.

Who's there?

Matthews.

Matthews Who?

Matthews are wet. Can I come in and dwy my thocks?

^^^^^^^^^^^^^^^^^^^^^^^^^^^^^^

Knock-knock.

Who's there?

Rhoda.

Rhoda Who?

Rhoda letter to my mama today.

Knock-knock.
Who's there?
Owl.
Owl Who?
Owl tell you if promise not to reveal my owdentity.

^^^^^^^^^^^^^^^^^^^^^^^^^^^^^^^

Knock-knock.
Who's there?
Lena.
Lena Who?
Lena little closer. I don't hear too good.

^^^^^^^^^^^^^

Knock-knock.
Who's there?
Watson.
Watson Who?
Watson the grill? I'm hungry.

Knock-knock.
Who's there?
Fido.
Fido Who?
Fido known you lived here, I'do come to visit sooner.

^^^^^^^^^^^^^^^^^^^^^^^^^^^^^^

Knock-knock.
Who's there?
Dishes.
Dishes Who?
Dishes Tommy, your besht friend. Don't you recognishe me?

^^^^^^^^^^^^^^^^^^^^^^^^^^^^^^

Knock-knock.
Who's there?
Samoa.
Samoa Who?
Samoa ice kweam, pwease.

Knock-knock.
  Who's there?
Sarah.
  Sarah Who?
Sarah good way for me to untie this knot?

^^^^^^^^^^^^^^^^^^^^^^^^^^^^^^

Knock-knock.
  Who's there?
Juneau.
  Juneau Who?
Juneau I was your next
door neighbor?

^^^^^^,

Knock-knock.
  Who's there?
Jamaica.
  Jamaica Who?
Jamaica hotdog for me if I asked you to?

Knock-knock.
Who's there?
Wendy.
Wendy Who?
Wendy come looking for me, tell them I'm not here.

^^^^^^^^^^^^^^^^^^^^^^^^^^^^^^

Knock-knock.
Who's there?
Celeste.
Celeste Who?
Celeste time I'll ever ask you to come out and play.

^^^^^^^^^^^^^^^^^^^^^^^^^^^^^^

Knock-knock.
Who's there?
Lettuce.
Lettuce Who?
Lettuce in! It's raining out here!

Knock-knock.
Who's there?
Ken.
Ken Who?
Ken you come out and play this afternoon?

∧∧∧∧∧∧∧∧∧∧∧∧∧∧∧∧∧∧∧∧∧∧∧∧∧∧∧∧∧

Knock-knock.
Who's there?
Bewitches.
Bewitches Who?
Bewitches in just a moment.

∧∧∧∧∧∧∧∧∧∧

Knock-knock.
Who's there?
Turnip.
Turnip Who?
Turnip the stereo,
please.

Knock-knock.
Who's there?
Sherwood.
Sherwood Who?
Sherwood like to play with y'all this afternoon.

^^^^^^^^^^^^^^^^^^^^^^^^^^^^^^^^

Knock-knock.
Who's there?
Sam.
Sam Who?
Sam times I think you don't love me like I love you.

^^^^^^^^^^^^^^^^^^^^^^^^^^^^^^^^

Knock-knock.
Who's there?
Police.
Police Who?
Police open the door.

Knock-knock.
  Who's there?
Kenya.
  Kenya Who?
Kenya gimme a dollar to buy an ice cream cone?

∧∧∧∧∧∧∧∧∧∧∧∧∧∧∧∧∧∧∧∧∧∧∧∧∧∧∧∧

Knock-knock.
  Who's there?
Jess.
  Jess Who?
Jess open the door and don't ask questions.

∧∧∧∧∧∧∧∧∧∧

Knock-knock.
  Who's there?
Annette.
  Annette Who?
Annette catches more
fish than a hook.

Knock-knock.
  Who's there?
Anita.
  anita Who?
Anita flashlight so I can see in the dark.

^^^^^^^^^^^^^^^^^^^^^^^^^^^^

Knock, Knock.
  Who's there?
Thumping.
  Thumping Who?
Thumping fuzzy and gross is crawling down your back.

^^^^^^^^^^^^^^^^^^^^^^^^^^^^

Knock-knock.
  Who's there?
noise.
  noise Who?
noise day, isn't it?

Knock-knock.
Who's there?
Alaska.
Alaska Who?
Alaska my dad if I can come out to play.

^^^^^^^^^

Knock-knock.
Who's there?
Stan.
Stan Who?
Stan back. I'm coming in.

^^^^^^^^^

Knock-knock.
Who's there?
Max.
Max Who?
Max me hungry just smellin'
those hamburgers on the
grill.

Knock-knock.
    Who's there?
Telephone.
    Telephone Who?
Telephone company they've made a mistake on our long-distance bill.

^^^^^^^^^^^^^^^^^^^^^^^^^^^^^

Knock-knock.
    Who's there?
Dishwashing.
    Dishwashing Who?
Dishwashing the way I ushed to shpeak before I losht my two front teeth.

^^^^^^^^^^^^^^^^^^^^^^^^^^^^^

Knock-knock.
    Who's there?
Abyssinia.
    Abyssinia Who?
Abyssinia in church Sunday.

Knock-knock.
Who's there?
Theresa.
Theresa Who?
Theresa thunderstorm coming up; close the windows.

^^^^^^^^^^^^^^^^^^^^^^^^^^^^^

Knock-knock.
Who's there?
Moscow.
Moscow Who?
Moscow is brown and pa's cow is black with horns.

^^^^^^^^^

Knock-knock.
Who's there?
Sam the drummer.
Beat it.

Knock-knock.
Who's there?
Adolph.
Adolph Who?
Adolph ball just came in the window.

∧∧∧∧∧∧∧∧∧∧∧∧∧∧∧∧∧∧∧∧∧∧∧∧∧∧∧

Knock-knock.
Who's there?
Pudding.
Pudding Who?
Just pudding the final touches on painting your door.

∧∧∧∧∧∧∧∧∧∧∧∧∧∧∧∧∧∧∧∧∧∧∧∧∧∧∧

Knock-knock.
Who's there?
Warts.
Warts Who?
Warts the difference between frogs and toads?

MUSIC

Adam: "I crossed a dog with a piano student."
Vera: "What did you get?"
Adam: "A dog whose bark was worse than her bite."

^^^^^^^^^^^^^^^^^^^^^^^^^^^^^^^^

Claire: "Those are cute bongos you have for earrings. They're so tiny! Can you really play them?"
Brittany: "Yes. Those are my ear drums."

Who was the spiciest rock 'n' roll singer of
    all time?
Elvis Parsley.

∧∧∧∧∧∧∧∧∧∧∧∧∧∧∧∧∧∧∧∧∧∧∧∧∧∧∧∧

Patrice: "What's a hobo?"
Nicole: "I think it's a wind instrument."

∧∧∧∧∧∧∧∧∧∧∧∧∧∧∧∧∧∧∧∧∧∧∧∧∧∧∧∧

Meredith: "I've been playing the piano for
    five years now."
Ethan: "Do you ever stop to go to the bath-
    room?"

∧∧∧∧∧∧∧∧∧∧∧∧∧∧∧∧∧∧∧∧∧∧∧∧∧∧∧∧

Sheila: "Why does Francis Scott Key get
    credit for 'The Star-Spangled Banner'? "
Richie: "I guess because he learned all the
    words before anyone else."

Why was the lemon banned from the orchestra?
It hit too many sour notes.

∧∧∧∧∧∧∧∧∧∧∧∧∧∧∧∧∧∧∧∧∧∧∧∧∧∧∧∧∧∧

What did the pianist do after his wrists developed carpal tunnel syndrome?
Played by ear.

∧∧∧∧∧∧∧∧∧∧∧∧

What brass instrument is twice as large as a tuba?
A fourba.

∧∧∧∧∧∧∧∧∧∧∧∧

Erskine: "I think I need to clean my tuba."
Band director: "Try this tuba toothpaste."

How do you keep your arm from going to
    sleep?
Wear a singing wristwatch.

∧∧∧∧∧∧∧∧∧∧∧∧∧∧∧∧∧∧∧∧∧∧∧∧∧∧∧∧

Patient: "I've swallowed my harmonica."
Doctor: "Good thing you don't play the
    guitar."

∧∧∧∧∧∧∧∧∧∧∧∧∧∧∧∧∧∧∧∧∧∧∧∧∧∧∧∧

"I know a woman who can sing alto and
soprano at the same time."
  "How does she do that?"
  "She has two heads."

∧∧∧∧∧∧∧∧∧∧∧∧∧∧∧∧∧∧∧∧∧∧∧∧∧∧∧∧

What's a geologist's favorite kind of music?
Rock.

Clive: "It sure was an interesting symphony
  concert last night. The tuba player's wig
  slid off into the bell of his horn!"
Harry: "Oh, no! Did they stop the concert?"
Clive: "No. He just blew his top and went
  right on playing."

∧∧∧∧∧∧∧∧∧∧∧∧

Steven: "I wish
  you sang only
  Christmas
  carols."
Mickey: "Why?"
Steven: "Then
  I'd have to
  listen to you only
  one month out
  of the year."

OCCUPATIONS

Reporter: "Do you like
    your job, sir?"
Astronomer: "Yes. It's
    heavenly."

^^^^^^^^^^^^^

How do preachers communicate with
each other?
Parson to parson.

^^^^^^^^^^^^^^^^^^^^^^^^^^^^^

Where do FBI agents go on vacation?
Club Fed.

OCEANS & RIVERS

Albert: "Do you know what happens when you throw a gray rock into the Red Sea?"

Lon: "It changes color?"

Albert: "No, it gets wet."

^^^^^^^^^^^^^^^^^^^^^^^^^^^^^^^^

What was Moby Dick's favorite dinner?

Fish and ships.

The Cantrell family was vacationing aboard a Mississippi River steamboat.

"Is it true," little brother asked the steamboat captain, "that you know every stump and snag on the whole Mississippi River?"

"I sure do," the captain boasted.

Just then the boat ran up on a snag and stopped abruptly.

"There's one," the captain said.

PLAYING

Jacqui strolled into the kitchen with a brand-new baseball.

"Where did you get that?" her mother asked.

"Outside. It was lost."

"Now, Jacqui, are you sure it was lost?"

"Yeah, I saw the boy down the street looking for it."

∧∧∧∧∧∧∧∧∧∧∧∧∧∧∧∧∧∧∧∧∧∧∧∧∧∧∧∧∧

Mother: "Charlie, why aren't you playing ball with your friends?"

Charlie: "Every time it's my turn, they change the rules."

Bart: "Your nose is red. You must've been in the sun too long at the beach yesterday."
Shane: "No I wasn't. I was bobbing for French fries."

^^^^^^^^^^^^^^^^^^^^^^^^^^^^^^

Swimmer: "Are there any sharks in this bay?"
Lifeguard: "Not anymore. The crocodiles got 'em."

^^^^^^^^^^^^^^^^^^^^^^^^^^^^^^

A mother came home to find the living room window broken.

"Joel," she called to her son, "do you know anything about this window?"

"Well," Joel said, "I was cleaning my sling-shot and it went off accidentally."

RESTAURANTS

Marsha: "Did you hear about the new café in Paris that sells bag lunches?"
Amy: "No. What's it called?"
Marsha: "The Lunch Bag of Notre Dame."

^^^^^^^^^^^^^^^^^

Walker: "This is not a very good restaurant. I just found a bone."
Suzette: "In your soup?"
Walker: "No, in my lasagna."

What's the best way for a guy to propose to a gal at a fast-food restaurant?
With an onion ring.

^^^^^^^^^^^^^^^^^^^^^^^^^^^^^^^

Waitress: "Would you like for me to cut your pizza into four pieces or eight?"
Dawn: "Four. We'd never finish eight."

^^^^^^^^^^^^^^^^^^^^^^^^^^^^^^^

Waiter: "Did you enjoy your bison steaks?"
Dining family, in unison: "Yes, we enjoyed them very much!"
Waiter: "Good. Here's your buffalo bill."

^^^^^^^^^^^^^^^^^^^^^^^^^^^^^^^

Amy: "Did you know NASA has opened a café on the surface of the moon?"
Marsha: "Yeah. I heard it has no atmosphere to speak of."

Rich diner: "What's the most expensive soup you have on the menu?"
Waitress: "The one with six carrots in it."

^^^^^^^^^^^^^^^^^^^^^^^^^^^^^^^

A dog walked into a restaurant, sat down at a table, and ordered a cup of coffee.

"That'll be one dollar," the waitress said when she brought the coffee. She added, "You're the first dog I've ever served coffee."

"And at one dollar a cup," said the dog, "I'm sure I'll be the last."

^^^^^^^^^^

Who was the restaurant's star waiter?
Souperman.

It was almost closing time, and the ice cream parlor was running very low on supplies when a crowd of teenagers came in after a soccer game.

"What flavors do you have?" asked one.

"Chocolate, vanilla, strawberry, peach, and cherry," said the clerk. "And you can have any one you want, as long as it's vanilla."

^^^^^^^^^^^^^^^^^^^^^^^^^^^^^^^^^^^

Two girls went into a fast-food restaurant late one night.

"Have you got anymore cheeseburgers?" asked one.

"Sure," said the clerk.

"Then why did you make so many?"

RIDDLES

What's the most successful thing government has ever invented?
The postage stamp, because it always sticks to its task until completion.

^^^^^^^^^^^^^^^^^^^^^^^^^^^^^^^^^

Teacher: "If four people are standing beneath one umbrella, how many do you think will get wet?"
Student: "Depends on whether it's raining."

What are ten things in life you can always
      count on?
Your fingers.

∧∧∧∧∧∧∧∧∧∧∧∧∧∧∧∧∧∧∧∧∧∧∧∧∧∧∧∧∧

What kind of ears do you find on a train
      engine?
Engineers.

∧∧∧∧∧∧∧∧∧∧∧∧∧∧∧∧∧∧∧∧∧∧∧∧∧∧∧∧∧

What can you break just by calling its name?
Silence.

∧∧∧∧∧∧∧∧∧∧∧∧∧∧∧∧∧∧∧∧∧∧∧∧∧∧∧∧∧

Jim was three years old on his last birthday
      and will be five years old on his next
      birthday. How can that be?
Today is his fourth birthday.

What never asks questions but gets a lot of
    answers?
A doorbell.

^^^^^^^^^^^^^^^^^^^^^^^^^^^^^

What word contains three *e*'s but only one
    letter?
Envelope.

^^^^^^^^^

What always seems to
    be behind time?
A clock face.

^^^^^^^^

Why are mush-
    rooms shaped
    like umbrellas?
*Because they grow in
    damp places.*

What is cut and spread out on the table but never eaten?
A deck of cards.

∧∧∧∧∧∧∧∧∧∧∧∧∧∧∧∧∧∧∧∧∧∧∧∧∧∧∧

How do seven cousins divide five potatoes?
Mash them.

∧∧∧∧∧∧∧∧∧∧∧∧∧∧∧∧∧∧∧∧∧∧∧∧∧∧∧

What word in the English language is usually pronounced wrong even by scholars?
Wrong.

∧∧∧∧∧∧∧∧∧∧∧∧∧∧∧∧∧∧∧∧∧∧∧∧∧∧∧

Teacher: "If the plural of man is men, and the plural of woman is women, what is the plural of child?"
Student: "Twins."

Denise: "I know a man who shaves a dozen times a day."
Lindy: "Who in the world is that?"
Denise: "The barber."

∧∧∧∧∧∧∧∧∧∧∧∧∧∧∧∧∧∧∧∧∧∧∧∧∧∧∧∧∧

What button will you never lose?
Your belly button.

∧∧∧∧∧∧∧∧∧∧∧

What's the best relief for ingrown toe-nails?
Ingrown toes.

∧∧∧∧∧∧∧∧∧∧

Why do skeletons stay home every night?
They have no body to go out with.

Why are ice cubes kept in the freezer?
To keep the freezer cold.

∧∧∧∧∧∧∧∧∧∧∧∧∧∧∧∧∧∧∧∧∧∧∧∧∧∧∧

What's long, sharp, and one-eyed?
A needle.

∧∧∧∧∧∧∧∧∧∧∧∧∧∧∧∧∧∧∧∧∧∧∧∧∧∧∧

Why were the ten toes nervous?
They were being followed by two heels.

∧∧∧∧∧∧∧∧∧∧∧∧∧∧∧∧∧∧∧∧∧∧∧∧∧∧∧

What's the tiniest room you'll ever find?
A mushroom.

∧∧∧∧∧∧∧∧∧∧∧∧∧∧∧∧∧∧∧∧∧∧∧∧∧∧∧

Which month has twenty-eight days?
All twelve of them.

What vegetable is a plumber's best friend?
a leek.

^^^^^^^^^^^^^^^^^^^^^^^^^^^^^^^

What gets larger if you take anything away
from it?
a hole.

^^^^^^^^^^^^^^^^^^^^^^^^^^^^^

What has a fork and a
mouth, but never
eats food?
a river.

^^^^^^^^^^^

How is an apple like
a pair of roller
skates?
*Both have caused the
fall of humans.*

What did one math teacher say to the
    other?
I've got a problem.

^^^^^^^^^^^^^^^^^^^^^^^^^^^^^^^

Before the discovery of Australia, what was
    the earth's largest island?
Australia.

^^^^^^^^^^^^^^^^^^^^^^^^^^^^^^^

What's the noblest item ever made from a
    piece of wood?
A ruler.

SCHOOL

Geography teacher: "Copley, can you tell me where Amsterdam is?"
Copley: "Er—here it is! Page 75!"

^^^^^^^^^^^^^^^^^^^^^^^^^^^^

Where do numbers take a bath?
In mathtubs.

^^^^^^^^^^^^^^^^^^^^^^^^^^^^

Teacher: "What are zebras good for?"
Student: "To illustrate the letter *z.*"

Literature teacher: "Otto, can you tell us who Homer was?"

Otto: "He was Mickey Mantle's sidekick."

^^^^^^^^^^^^^^^^^^^^^^^^^^^^^^^

Teacher: "Do you think it was just as easy to explore the Arctic as it was Antarctica?"

Student: "I don't know. . . . There's a world of difference."

^^^^^^^^^^^^^^^^^^^^^^^^^^^^^^^

Teacher: "How can one child make so many mistakes in one day?"

Student: "By getting up early."

^^^^^^^^^^^^^^^^^^^^^^^^^^^^^^^

Teacher: "Everyone write down the number eleven."

Student: "Which one comes first?"

A little boy walked up to the teacher's desk and said, "Miss Phillips, I've got bad news for you."

"What is it?" asked Miss Phillips.

"I'm afraid you're in big trouble."

"And why is that?"

"Well, my father says if my grades don't pick up, somebody's in for a beating."

^^^^^^^^^^^^^^^^^^^^^^^^^^^^^^

What's the capital of Wyoming?
That's easy:
   W.

^^^^^^

Teacher: "What do you call a star with a tail?"
Student: "Mickey Mouse!"

When little Josie came home from her first day at school, her mother asked, "So how do you like school, Josie?"

"Closed," Josie said.

^^^^^^^^^^^^^^^^^^^^^^^^^^^^^^^^^

Andy: "The teacher sure kept me busy today."
Michelle: "What was your assignment?"
Andy: "She put me in a round room and told me to sit in the corner."

^^^^^^^^^^^^^^^^^^^^^^^^^^^^^^^^^

Why did Jerome go to night school?
So he could learn to read in the dark.

^^^^^^^^^^^^^^^^^^^^^^^^^^^^^^^^^

What does a schoolteacher have in common with an eye doctor?
They both stare at pupils.

Teacher: "Have you ever read much Shakespeare before now?"
New student: "I don't think so. Who wrote it?"

^^^^^^^^^^^^^^^^^^^^^^

Teacher: "You didn't answer the last two questions on the test."
Student: "Oh. Well, the answers are stuck inside my fountain pen."

^^^^^^^^^^^^^^^^^^^^^

Lila arrived for her second day of first grade carrying a ladder.
"What's the ladder for?" asked a friend.
"I'm ready for high school," Lila said.

What's more difficult than cutting school?
Taping it back together.

^^^^^^^^^^^^^^^^^^^^^^^^^^^^^^

Ken: "What are you looking for?"
Kelley: "My earring."
Ken: "I'll help. Where do you think you lost it?"
Kelley: "Down in the science lab."
Ken: "Then why in the world are we looking for it here in the lunchroom?"
Kelley: "The light's much brighter in here."

^^^^^^^^^^^^^^^^^^^^^^^^^^^^^^

Teacher: "Why haven't you turned in your homework?"
Student: "I accidentally used the paper to make a paper airplane."
Teacher: "Where's the airplane?"
Student: "Somebody skyjacked it."

Teacher: "Jory, what do you think of
   Shakespeare's writings?"
Jory: "I think much of what he wrote was a
   dreadful tragedy."

^^^^^^^^^^^^^^^^^^^^^^^^^^^^^^^

Did you hear about the schoolteacher who was so
   suspicious while giving
   tests that his eyes
   watched each
   other?

^^^^^^^

Perry: "Your
   lunch
   box has a
   glass top. That's neat!"
Tammy: "Yes. When I'm
   on the bus, I can easily
   tell whether I'm going to school or going
   home."

Teacher: "Warren, can you spell
    'Mississippi'?"
Warren: "Do you want me to spell the state
    or the river?"

∧∧∧∧∧∧∧∧∧∧∧∧∧∧∧∧∧∧∧∧∧∧∧∧∧∧∧

First-grade teacher: "Hubie, what comes
    after g?"
Hubie: "Whiz."

∧∧∧∧∧∧∧∧∧∧∧∧∧∧∧∧∧∧∧∧∧∧∧∧∧∧∧

Teacher: "You missed school yesterday,
    didn't you?"
Arnold: "No, not much."

∧∧∧∧∧∧∧∧∧∧∧∧∧∧∧∧∧∧∧∧∧∧∧∧∧∧∧

Teacher: "Are you having trouble with the
    test questions?"
Student: "Just with the answers."

Wally: "I heard you had to stay in at recess. Did the teacher make you write the same sentence over and over?"

Henry: "No. She kept me busy, though."

Wally: "Doing what?"

Henry: "She gave me a piece of paper that said 'See other side.' "

Wally: "So what did it say on the other side?"

Henry: "That side said 'See other side,' too."

∧∧∧∧∧∧∧.

A student drew a picture of a stage coach with no wheels.
"What holds it up?" asked the teacher.
"Outlaws."

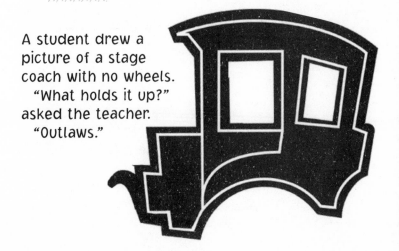

Mother: "What did you learn in school today?"

Elena: "We learned to say 'Yes, Ma'am' and 'Yes, Sir.' "

Mother: "That's wonderful! You'll remember it, won't you?"

Elena: "Yeah, I guess."

^^^^^^^^^^^^^^^^^^^^^^^^^^^^^^

Teacher: "Why is Chicago time behind Boston time?"

Student: "Because Boston was discovered first."

^^^^^^^^^^^^^^^^^^^^^^^^^^^^^^

Teacher: "Name three important things that have occurred in the past twenty-five years."

Rodger: "The space shuttle, the end of the Iron Curtain. . .and me!"

Teacher: "How many seconds in a minute?"
Don: "Sixty."
Teacher: "That's right. So how many seconds in an hour."
Don, after a long calculation: "Three-thousand, six-hundred."
Teacher: "Very good! Now, this is a hard one: How many seconds in a year?"
Don: "Twelve."
Teacher: "Twelve? How do you get that?"
Don: "January 2nd, February 2nd, March 2nd. . ."

∧∧∧∧∧∧∧∧∧∧∧∧∧∧∧∧∧∧∧/

"Teacher, I just swallowed my fountain pen!" George screamed.

"Then you may finish the test with your pencil."

What's the favorite drink of cheerleaders?
Root beer.

^^^^^^^^^^^^^^^^^^^^^^^^^^^^^^^

Teacher: "Kenny, compose a sentence using
the word 'archaic.' "
Kenny: "We all know we can't have archaic
and eat it, too."

^^^^^^^^^^^^^^^^^^^^^^^^^^^^^^^

When do leaves start to turn?
The night before a big test.

^^^^^^^^^^^^^^^^^^^^^^^^^^^^^^^

The teacher asked Marie, "Please go to the
map and locate Cuba."
Marie quickly found Cuba on the map at
the front of the room.
"That's good, Marie. Now class, can anyone
tell me who discovered Cuba?"
Derek quickly raised his hand. "Marie!"

Teacher: "In the Old West, what was cow-
    hide mainly used for?"
Student: "To keep the cow in one piece?"

∧∧∧∧∧∧∧∧∧∧∧∧∧∧∧∧∧∧∧∧∧∧∧∧∧∧∧∧∧∧

Teacher: "Are you chewing gum?"
New student: "No, I'm Alison."

∧∧∧∧∧∧∧∧∧∧∧∧∧∧∧∧∧

Teacher: "If you found a
    dollar in your left
    trousers pocket
    and sixty-five
    cents in your
    right pocket,
    what would you
    have?"
Student: "Somebody
    else's britches."

Virgil: "How do you spell 'telephone'? "
Shana: "T-e-l-e-p-h-o-n-e. If you would read
    the dictionary, you would know
    that yourself."
Virgil: "Hmm. I don't think I want to read
    the dictionary. I'll wait for the movie."

∧∧∧∧∧∧∧∧∧∧∧∧∧∧∧∧∧∧∧∧∧∧∧∧∧∧∧∧∧

Nina came home from school and told her
mother, "Our teachers talk to themselves
too much."

    "Really? Do you think they realize it?"

    "Nah. They think students are listening to
them."

Teacher: "Robert, how do you spell 'elevate'?"

Robert: "E-l-a-v-a-t."

Teacher: "No, that's not the way it's spelled in the dictionary."

Robert: "You asked me how I spelled it, not the dictionary."

SCIENCE

Meg: "Did you know there are more than a thousand miles of blood vessels in the human body?"

Peg: "Really? No wonder my dad complains of tired blood."

∧∧∧∧∧∧∧∧∧∧∧∧∧∧∧∧∧∧∧∧∧∧∧∧∧∧∧∧∧∧

"How did the new satellite pictures of California turn out?" one NASA scientist asked another.

"Not so good," said the other. "Someone moved."

Teacher: "What's the difference between air and water?"
Student: "Air can get wetter. Water can't."

^^^^^^^^^^^^^^^^^^^^^^^^^^^^^^^

Teacher: "Who was the first brother to fly an airplane at Kitty Hawk, North Carolina? Was it Orville or Wilbur?"

"Orville!" shouted one student.

"Wilbur!" shouted another.

"They're both Wright," said a third.

^^^^^

Where do stars and planets go to school? *At the universe-ity.*

Why were the Wright Brothers first in flight?
Because they weren't wrong.

^^^^^^^^^^^^^^^^^^^^^^^^^^^^^^^

"I didn't understand the science teacher's
lesson about the sky today," said Jan.
    "Why not?" asked her father.
    "It was way over my head."

^^^^^^^^^^^^^^^^^^^^^^^^^^^^^^^

What do you call four-day-old pizza?
A science project.

SLEEP

"I can't go to sleep at night," complained Ardie.

"Have you tried counting sheep?" asked Mardie.

"How will that help?"

"It'll bore you and you'll fall asleep."

A few days later, Mardie asked, "Have you been able to sleep?"

"Nope," said Ardie.

"Did you try counting sheep?"

"Yep. I got up to 3,628."

"Then what happened?"

"Well, then it was time to get up."

"What are you doing in front of the mirror with your eyes closed?"

"I've always wondered what I look like when I'm asleep."

^^^^^^^^^^^^^^^^^^^^^^^^^^^^^^^^^^^^^

What happens if you sleep with a bar of soap under your pillow?
You'll slip out of bed in the morning.

SPORTS

Hoyt: "I think sports are boring."

Bonnie: "Why do you think so?"

Hoyt: "I can always tell you the score before the game even begins."

Bonnie: "Really?"

Hoyt: "Sure. It's 0 to 0."

^^^^^^^^^^^^^^^^^^^^^^^^^^^^^^^^^

What do four balls mean in baseball?
They mean you can lose three and still be okay.

Why do golfers carry extra socks?
In case they get a hole in one.

∧∧∧∧∧∧∧∧∧∧∧∧∧∧∧∧∧∧∧∧∧∧∧∧∧∧∧∧∧

Harry: "Who was the first golfer in history?"
Sherry: "I don't know. Sam Snead?"
Harry: "No—Magellan. He went around in
     1519."

∧∧∧∧∧∧∧∧∧∧∧∧∧∧∧∧∧∧∧∧∧∧∧∧∧∧∧∧∧

What did the SCUBA diver find quaking at
     the bottom of the bay?
A nervous wreck.

∧∧∧∧∧∧∧∧∧∧∧∧∧∧∧∧∧∧∧∧∧∧∧∧∧∧∧∧∧

Coach: "So you think you know everything
     there is to know about soccer?"
New player: "I do."
Coach: "Then how many holes are in the
     goal net?"

"You'll never make the basketball team," said Herman. "You're too short."

"But maybe," said Hank, "I could lie about my height."

∧∧∧∧∧∧∧∧∧∧∧∧∧∧∧∧∧∧∧∧∧∧∧∧∧∧∧∧∧∧∧

Reporter: "Why are you a skydiver? Isn't it extremely dangerous jumping out of airplanes?"
Skydiver: "No, jumping is a piece of cake—but it does get risky as you approach the ground."

∧∧∧∧∧∧∧∧∧∧∧∧∧∧∧∧∧∧∧∧

Why do hockey players spend all their time on ice?
Because their skates would bog down in the sand.

STATES

"What's your name?"
"Tex."
"You're from Texas?"
"Nope, Connecticut. I don't like being called 'Con.'"

‸‸‸‸‸‸‸‸‸‸‸‸‸

Rachel: "Did you know the USA has four new states?"
Shelby: "You mean, besides Hawaii and Alaska?"
Rachel: "Yes—New Hampshire, New Jersey, New Mexico, and New York."

TELEPHONES

"This phone cord's too long," a woman said. "I'm always tripping over it. See what you can do to fix it."

So her husband called the phone company. "Our phone cord's too long," he said. "Pull in about five feet of slack, please."

^^^^^^^^^^^^^^^^^^^^^^^^^^^^^^^^^^^^

Why didn't Josie pay her telephone bill?
She believed in free speech.

What happens when you dial 116?
*The ambulance rushes to your house upside
down.*

^^^^^^^^^^^^^^^^^^^^^^^^^^^^^^^^

"Charity, please answer the phone for me!"
Mother told Charity.

"Sure," Charity said, running to grab the
receiver. "Hello, phone."

^^^^^^^^^^^^^^^^^^^^^^^^^^^^^^^^

"Did you know that certain people who are
almost deaf can still use the telephone?"
Erin asked.

"No," replied Joey, "but a lot of dumb people certainly use it."

TELEVISION & RADIO

"Are you going to watch the eclipse of the moon tonight?"

"Depends on which channel. We don't get cable TV."

^^^^^^^^^^^^^^^^^^^^^^^^^^^^^^^^^

"My sister doesn't like our new computer."

"Why not?"

"It doesn't get the Disney Channel."

Why did Albert put his radio in the freezer?
He wanted to hear some cool music.

AAAAAAAAAAAAAAAAAAAAAAAAAAAAAA

Art: "Did you hear the concert on the radio last night?"
Keri: "My radio won't come on at night."
Art: "What's wrong with it?"
Keri: "It's an AM radio."

AAAAAAAAAAAAAAAAAAAAAAAAAAAAAA

Blair: "Sometimes I wonder about Kippie."
Dirk: "Why is that?"
Blair: "He tried to find the English Channel on cable TV."

VACATIONS

Henry: "Mom, why are we packing soap in the suitcase?"
Mom: "We'll need it for the trip."
Henry: "But I thought this was supposed to be a vacation."

∧∧∧∧∧∧∧∧∧∧∧∧∧∧∧∧∧∧∧∧∧∧∧∧∧∧∧∧∧∧

Brad: "I can get from Philadelphia to Baltimore without buying a ticket."
Joanna: "How?"
Brad: "Walk."

Nickie: "I've finally saved up enough money to go to Hawaii!"

Mickie: "Great! When are you going?"

Nickie: "As soon as I save up enough to get back."

^^^^^^^^^^^^^^^^^^^^^^^^^^^^^

A troop of Girl Scouts were huddling around a campfire. "Can bears see at night?" Cindy asked nervously.

"I reckon they have to," Wren suggested. "They aren't able to hold flashlights."

^^^^^^^^^^^^^^^^^^^^^^^^^^^^^

Randy and Andy visited the beach for the first time in their lives. "Wow! Look at all the water!" Randy shouted.

"Yeah—and that's only the surface!" Andy said.

Father: "Jack, why did you put a beetle in your sister's sleeping bag?"
Jack: "I couldn't find a snake."

^^^^^^^^^^^^^^^^^^^^^^^^^^^^^^^^^^^

Trail guide: "You don't have to worry about riding along those narrow mountain trails. These donkeys are sure-footed critters."
Tourist: "Does that mean when they kick, they don't miss?"

WHAT'S THAT?

What's black and shriveled up and giggles?

A ticklish raisin.

^^^^^^^^^^^^^^^^^^^^^^^^^^^^^^

What do you get when you cross a praying mantis with a termite?

An insect that gives thanks before eating your floors.

What do you call two bars of soap?
a pair of slippers.

∧∧∧∧∧∧∧∧∧∧∧∧∧∧∧∧∧∧∧∧∧∧∧∧∧∧∧∧∧∧

What's blue and red and headed for the
    doctor's office?
a tomato with frostbite.

∧∧∧∧∧∧∧∧

What says, "Tick-
    tock-ruff-ruff?"
a watchdog.

∧∧∧∧∧∧∧∧∧∧∧∧∧

What do you get when you
    cross a camel with a station
    wagon?
a camel that seats nine.

What's long and green and very dangerous?
A herd of charging cucumbers.

∧∧∧∧∧∧∧∧∧∧∧∧∧∧∧∧∧∧∧∧∧∧∧∧∧∧∧∧∧

What's purple and wears a mask?
The Lone Grape.

∧∧∧∧∧∧∧∧∧∧∧∧∧∧∧∧∧∧∧∧∧∧∧∧∧∧∧∧∧

What has one head and four legs?
A bed.

∧∧∧∧∧∧∧∧∧∧∧∧∧∧∧∧∧∧∧∧∧∧∧∧∧∧∧∧∧

What's long and slimy, swims, carries a
    submachine gun, and honks a horn?
An auto-mob-eel.

∧∧∧∧∧∧∧∧∧∧∧∧∧∧∧∧∧∧∧∧∧∧∧∧∧∧∧∧∧

What's the opposite of minimum?
Minipop.

What do you get when you cross a wood-pecker and a carrier pigeon?
A bird that knocks before delivering the message.

^^^^^^^^^^^^^^^^^^^^^^^^^^^^^^

What's long and yellow and helps elderly ladies across the street?
Banana Scouts.

^^^^^^^^^^

What do you get when you cross a parrot with a grizzly bear?
Whatever it is, if it says, "Polly wanna cracker," you better give it a whole box!

What's yellow, has four doors, and lies on its
    back?
A sick taxicab.

^^^^^^^^^^^^^^^^^^^^^^^^^^^^^^

What do you get when you cross a rooster
    and a bull?
Roost beef.

^^^^^^^^^^^^^^^^^^^^^^^^^^^^^^

What has three heads, two arms, two wings,
    eight legs, and two tails?
A horseback rider carrying a falcon.

^^^^^^^^^^^^^^^^^^^^^^^^^^^^^^

What animal sees just as well from one end
    as the other?
A blind one.

What's purple and goes, "Slam! Slam!"?
a two-door grape.

∧∧∧∧∧∧∧∧∧∧∧∧∧∧∧∧∧∧∧∧∧∧∧∧∧∧

What's hairy and sneezes?
a peach with a cold.

∧∧∧∧∧∧∧∧∧∧∧∧∧∧∧∧∧∧∧∧∧∧∧∧∧∧

What hops around holding up banks?
a robbit.

∧∧∧∧∧∧

What do you call a young fox after it's thiry days old?
Thirty-one days old.

WORK

"Did you hear Harry went to work at the bank?"

"No. Why does he want to work at a bank?"

"He heard there's money in it."

∧∧∧∧∧∧∧∧∧∧∧∧∧∧∧∧∧∧∧∧∧∧∧∧∧∧∧∧∧

Boss: "You drive nails like lightning."

Carpenter: "Pretty fast, huh?"

Boss: "Nope—you never hammer the same place twice."

Why did the weather announcer quit her
    job?
She didn't find the weather very agreeable.

^^^^^^^^^^^^^^^^^^^^^^^^^^^^

Will: "I just heard they
    aren't building rail-
    road tracks any
    longer."
Sam: "Why not?"
Will: "They're already
    long enough."

^^^^^^^^^^^^

Molly: "Why did your
    father go to work at
    the bakery?"
Allie: "He kneads the
    dough."

ODDS & ENDS

Why did Miriam put a bag of ice under her aunt's easy chair?

She wanted to see auntie freeze.

∧∧∧∧∧∧∧∧∧∧∧∧∧∧∧∧∧∧∧∧∧∧∧∧∧∧∧∧∧∧∧

Two walls were talking to each other when a man overheard them and shouted, "Be quiet!"

"Come on," one wall whispered softly to the other. "I'll meet you at the corner and we can finish our discussion."

Why won't a bicycle stand up when it's not
    moving?
It's two-tired.

^^^^^^^^^^^^^^^

Why did Lindy carry her
    umbrella to school?
*She didn't want to
    leave it home alone.*

^^^^^^^^^^^^

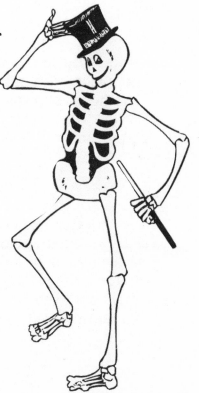

Morris: "Did you hear
    about the skeleton
    who became a
    movie star?"
Glenda: "How did he
    do that?"
Morris: "He had good
    connections."

Mother: "Has Clay finished changing that lightbulb yet?"

Billy: "I don't think so. He keeps breaking them accidentally with the hammer."

∧∧∧∧∧∧∧∧∧∧∧∧∧∧∧∧∧∧∧∧∧∧∧∧∧∧∧∧∧

Carey: "You sure have a weird name."

Bretopnius: "It's better than the one my father first pulled out of the hat."

Carey: "What was that?"

Bretopnius: "Eight-and-a-Quarter."

∧∧∧∧∧∧∧∧∧∧∧∧∧∧∧∧∧∧∧∧∧∧∧∧∧∧∧∧∧

Jamie's kitten had climbed high up a tree, and she said it wouldn't come down, no matter how long she coaxed. "What can we do?" she asked her father.

"Wait until September. He'll catch the first leaf that falls and float right to the ground."

What cowboy wears a black mask just like
the Lone Ranger's, rides a horse just like
Silver, and has a sidekick who could be
Tonto's twin brother?
The Clone Ranger.

∧∧∧∧∧∧∧∧∧∧∧∧∧∧∧∧∧∧∧∧∧∧∧∧∧∧∧∧∧

Winona: "Did you hear the McMillans are
moving to Gettysburg?"
Andrea: "No. Why are they moving?"
Winona: "Because
they want to have a
Gettysburg address."

∧∧∧∧∧∧∧∧∧∧∧

How did the cat
succeed in
winning a
starring role
in a movie?
With purr-sistence.

Part 2:

ANIMALS

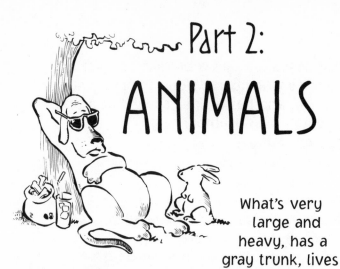

What's very large and heavy, has a gray trunk, lives in Scotland, and has baffled investigators for centuries?
The Loch Ness elephant.

^^^^^^^^^^^^^^^^^^^^^^^^^^^^^

What did one skunk say to the other?
"Let us spray."

^^^^^^^^^^^^^^^^^^^^^^^^^^^^^

What does a thiry-pound rat say?
"Here, kitty-kitty. . . ."

Will a poisonous snake die if it bites its tongue?

∧∧∧∧∧∧∧∧∧∧∧∧∧∧∧∧∧∧∧∧∧∧∧∧∧∧∧∧∧

"Oh, no! The weather forecaster is calling for rain!" the kangaroo groaned to the rabbit.

"What's the problem with that?" asked the rabbit. "We could use some rain."

"Yes, but that means my children will have to stay inside to play."

∧∧∧∧∧∧∧∧∧∧∧∧∧∧∧∧∧∧∧∧∧∧∧∧∧∧∧∧∧

What do you call a dozen rats?
Scary.

∧∧∧∧∧∧∧∧∧∧∧∧∧∧∧∧∧∧∧∧∧∧∧∧∧∧∧∧∧

What do you call a snake who gets elected mayor?
A civil serpent.

∧∧∧∧∧∧∧∧∧∧∧∧∧∧∧∧∧∧∧∧∧∧∧∧∧∧∧∧∧

Why do kangaroos paint themselves green?
So they can hide in a bowl of spinach.

Why do porcupines never lose games?
Because they always have more points than any other animal.

^^^^^^^^^^^^^^^^^^^^^^^^^^^^

What did one fox say to another?
"I'm tired of being hounded all the time."

^^^^^^^^^^^^^^^^^^^^^^^^^^^^

What do you call mouse shoes?
Squeakers.

^^^^^^^^^^^^^^^^^^^^^^^^^^^^

What did the boy porcupine say after he kissed the girl porcupine?
"Ouch!"

^^^^^^^^^^^^^^^^^^^^^^^^^^^^

"Do you think the skunk would be considered a very popular animal?" the teacher asked.

"Not exactly—but it's always the scenter of attention," the student answered.

"That's a beautiful new wool sweater you're wearing!" marveled Tammy. "It's so thick and warm! I wonder how many sheep it took to make a sweater that size."

"I don't know," said Rhonda. "Actually, I didn't know sheep could do handiwork."

∧∧∧∧∧∧∧∧∧∧∧∧∧∧∧∧∧∧∧∧∧∧∧∧∧∧∧

Why did the otter cross the road?
To get to the otter side.

∧∧∧∧∧∧∧∧∧∧∧∧∧∧∧∧∧∧∧∧∧∧∧∧∧∧∧

What do you call flying monkeys?
Hot-air baboons.

∧∧∧∧∧∧∧∧∧∧∧∧∧∧∧∧∧∧∧∧∧∧∧∧∧∧∧

What kind of infants prefer goat milk?
Infant goats.

∧∧∧∧∧∧∧∧∧∧∧∧∧∧∧∧∧∧∧∧∧∧∧∧∧∧∧

What do you call a rabbit with the sniffles?
a runny bunny.

How do mice keep their breath fresh all day long?
They rinse with mousewash.

^^^^^^^^^^^^^^^^^^^^^^^^^^^^

What's huge and gray and goes around in circles?
A hippopotamus in a revolving door.

^^^^^^^^^^^^^^^^^^^^^^^^^^^^

How did the chimpanzee break out of its cage?
With a monkey wrench.

^^^^^^^^^^^^^^^^^^^^^^^^^^^^

What animal looks a lot like an aardvark?
Another aardvark.

^^^^^^^^^^^^^^^^^^^^^^^^^^^^

What goes eighty miles an hour underground?
A prairie dog on a motorcycle.

A pair of zebras were wandering in Africa when they heard the thunderous sound of hooves over the horizon. A massive herd of giraffes appeared, running their way in a blinding cloud of dust. The zebras took cover behind a tree and waited for the giraffes to pass. Then they continued wandering.

A few hours later, another large herd of giraffes approached, stirring up a storm of dust. Again, the zebras got out of the way.

Near sundown, they found themselves in the path of a third mob of giraffes. Standing behind a rock, coughing from the thick dust as the tall animals rushed past, one zebra turned to the other and said, "I think we should move away. There's too much giraffic around here to suit me."

∧∧∧∧∧∧∧∧∧∧∧∧∧∧∧∧∧∧∧∧∧∧∧∧∧∧∧∧∧

What's the happiest animal in the wild?
The happypotamus.

Santa Claus was confused when he found three red-nosed reindeer as he prepared his sleigh. "What's this?" he asked Mrs. Claus. "Which one is Rudolph?"

Mrs. Claus wiped the noses of the three reindeer with her apron. Amazingly, only one red-nosed reindeer—the true Rudolph—remained.

"It's no real mystery," she explained. "Dancer and Prancer have been eating my cherry cobbler again."

^^^^^^^^^^^^^^^^^^^^^^^^^^^^^^^^^^^

When is the best time for a dog to come in the house?
When the door is open.

^^^^^^^^^^^^^^^^^^^^^^^^^^^^^^^^^^^

Why is it hard to talk to a ram?
He keeps butting in.

How does an elephant get out of a small car?
The same way he got in.

TONGUE TWISTER

The skunk sat on the stump.
The stump said the skunk stunk.
The skunk said the stump stunk.
Who stunk?

ARITHMETIC

"If you have 10 pieces of bubble gum and you give away 4, what do you have then?" the teacher asked.

"I have 6 pieces of gum and 4 new friends!" the student figured.

∧∧∧∧∧∧∧∧∧∧∧∧∧∧∧∧∧∧∧∧∧∧∧∧∧∧∧∧∧∧

Teacher: "Two trains are headed toward each other on the same track. They're both traveling 60 miles per hour, and they're 30 miles apart. How soon will they collide?"
Student: "Much too soon."

"My math teacher doesn't make sense," said Janet.

"Why do you think that?" asked Shayna.

"Yesterday she taught us that 9 plus 1 equals 10. Today she claims 7 plus 3 equals 10."

∧∧∧∧∧∧∧∧∧∧∧∧∧∧∧∧∧∧∧∧∧∧∧∧∧∧∧∧

Teacher: "Richie, if I offered you a choice between a basket with 36 bananas and a basket with 63 bananas, which would you choose?"

Richie: "The basket with 36 bananas."

Teacher: "Now Richie, surely you know 63 is more than 36."

Richie: "Yes, ma'am. That's why I'd pick the first basket. I can't stand bananas."

∧∧∧∧∧∧∧∧∧∧∧∧∧∧∧∧∧∧∧∧∧∧∧∧∧∧∧∧

Where do math teachers prefer to operate? *On multiplication tables.*

"Mom, how far away is the moon?" the little boy asked.

"About 240,000 miles."

"How far away is the ocean?"

"Well, the nearest one to us is the Pacific Ocean. That's about 500 miles from here, as the crow flies."

"Is the moon as big as the Pacific Ocean?"

"I'm not sure. The moon is roughly 2,000 miles in diameter, and the Pacific Ocean is about that far across, at the widest part. So I suppose in a way, you might say they're sort of the same size."

The little boy thought about that for a while, then asked one more question. "Well, how far away is Phoenix?"

"By car, Phoenix is about 120 miles from us."

The boy shook his head. "I don't get it at all. The moon is a quarter of a million miles away, and I can see the moon clearly at night. But I can't see Phoenix, 120 miles from here. I can't even see the Pacific Ocean."

AUTOMOBILES

"This car has never been involved in a wreck," assured the auto salesman.

"It *is* a wreck," said the wise customer.

∧∧∧∧∧∧∧∧∧∧∧∧∧∧∧∧∧∧∧∧∧∧∧∧∧∧∧∧∧∧∧

"Why are you wearing your winter coat?"

"I'm waxing my car."

"Why do you need a winter coat to wax a car?"

"The wax container says a heavy coat makes the shine last longer."

"Dad, why don't we park our car on the street?"

"Because we have a driveway. The car's safer there. That's what driveways are for."

"If it's for parking cars, then why do we call it a driveway?"

∧∧∧∧∧∧∧∧∧∧∧∧∧∧∧∧∧∧∧∧∧∧∧∧∧∧∧∧

What did the driver say when she came to a fork in the road?
"This must be the place to eat."

∧∧∧∧∧∧∧∧∧∧∧∧∧∧∧∧∧∧∧∧∧∧∧∧∧∧∧∧

What kind of rabbits are good at fixing flat tires?
Jackrabbits.

∧∧∧∧∧∧∧∧∧∧∧∧∧∧∧∧∧∧∧∧∧∧∧∧∧∧∧∧

"How did your dog get that nasty lump on it's head?" asked Sam.

"It was chasing a parked car," said Tom.

"My dad rides to work in a carpool."

"What does that mean?"

"I'm not sure. I think it's what happens when it rains and they have the top down."

TONGUE TWISTER

Moses supposes his toeses are roses,
But Moses supposes erroneously.
For nobody's toeses are poses of roses.
As Moses supposes his toeses to be.

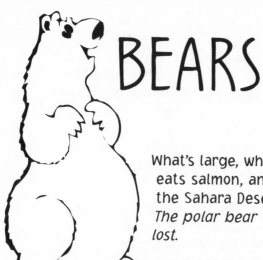

BEARS

What's large, white, fierce, eats salmon, and lives in the Sahara Desert?
The polar bear that got lost.

^^^^^^^^^^^^^^^^

Where do bears like to stay when they go on vacation?
At cave-inns.

^^^^^^^^^^^^^^^^^^^^^^^^^^^^^^^

"My feet are sore," one bear said to another. "I'm going to the mall to buy tennis shoes."

"What for?" asked his friend. "You're still going to have bear feet."

Brad: "Why do bears paint their faces yellow?"
Lad: "Don't know."
Brad: "So they can hide in banana trees."
Lad: "Impossible. I've never seen a bear in a banana tree."
Brad: "That's because they've painted their faces yellow."

∧∧∧∧∧∧∧∧∧∧∧∧∧∧∧∧∧∧∧∧∧∧∧∧∧∧

What's black and white, black and white, black and white?
A panda bear rolling down the mountain.

∧∧∧∧∧∧∧∧∧∧∧∧∧∧∧∧∧∧∧∧∧∧∧∧∧∧

Where do bears get their news?
From cub reporters.

∧∧∧∧∧∧∧∧∧∧∧∧∧∧∧∧∧∧∧∧∧∧∧∧∧∧

Why does a bear sleep three months out of the year?
No one is brave enough to wake it up.

"Someone's been eating my soup!" shouted Papa Bear.

"Someone's been eating my soup!" shouted Mama Bear.

"Hooray!" shouted Baby Bear. "Does that mean we can have ice cream for supper?"

^^^^^^^^^^^^^^^^^^^^^^^^^^^^^^^^

"Someone's been eating my soup!" yelled Papa Bear, finding his bowl empty at the supper table.

"And someone's been eating my soup!" yelled Baby Bear. His bowl was empty, too.

"Stop fussing," said Mama Bear. "I'm still cooking it."

TONGUE TWISTER

The boat floated forty fathoms.
Forty fathoms floated the boat.

BIBLE JOKES

"Who was the fastest runner in history?" asked Shelley.

"Adam," said Mackie. "The Bible says he was first in the human race."

^^^^^^^^^^^^^^^^^^^^^^^^^^^^^^^

What did Noah do for a living?
He was an ark-itect.

^^^^^^^^^^^^^^^^^^^^^^^^^^^^^^^

Science teacher: "Who discovered oxygen?"
Student: "Adam."

"Why does God create all humans as babies?" asked Bob. "Why doesn't He just go ahead and make us adults?"

"I suppose it's because babies take less material," suggested Toby.

∧∧∧∧∧∧∧∧∧∧∧∧∧∧∧∧∧∧∧∧∧∧∧∧∧∧∧∧

"Do you think the worms on Noah's ark were allowed to live inside apples?" asked Gigi.

"Oh, no," said Honi. "They had to be in pairs, remember?"

∧∧∧∧∧∧∧∧∧∧∧∧∧∧∧∧∧∧∧∧∧∧∧∧∧∧∧∧

"Does God hear everything in the world?" asked a Sunday school student.

"Yes," the teacher said, "every sound."

"All at one time?"

"Yes."

"Wow. His ears must be hurting from all that noise on the radio."

When do we first read of baseball in the Bible?
Genesis 1:1. It starts, "In the Big Inning. . ."

∧∧∧∧∧∧∧∧∧∧∧∧∧∧∧∧∧∧∧∧∧∧∧∧∧∧∧

"Mom and Dad say we can't go to the zoo today," sighed Barbie.
  "I have an idea," suggested Joan. "We can go over their heads. Let's pray!"

∧∧∧∧∧∧∧∧∧∧∧∧∧∧∧∧∧∧∧∧∧∧∧∧∧∧∧

Sunday school teacher: "Who was Noah's wife?"
Student: "Er. . .Joan of Ark?"

∧∧∧∧∧∧∧∧∧∧∧∧∧∧∧∧∧∧∧∧∧∧∧∧∧∧∧

Who was the most popular Old Testament actor?
Samson, who brought down the house.

BIRDS

Why did the songbird go
to the doctor?
To be tweeted.

∧∧∧∧∧∧∧∧∧∧∧∧/

What did the starving parrot say?
"Polly wanna CHEESEBURGER!"

∧∧∧∧∧∧∧∧∧∧∧∧∧∧∧∧∧∧∧∧∧∧∧∧∧∧∧

Amanda went to the pet store and told the clerk, "I want a BIG bag of bird seed."

"You must be planning to feed a lot of sparrows," said the clerk.

"No, actually, I'm planning to dye the seed blue and plant a BIG crop of bluebirds."

Why does the egret stand on one leg?
Because if it lifts the leg, it falls.

How high is the sky?
*High enough that birds don't have to
    worry about bumping their heads.*

What is a bird's favorite food?
Chocolate chirp cookies.

Teacher: "What kinds of birds are commonly
found in jungles?"
Student: "Hot, sweaty birds."

"My parakeet has proposed marriage," said
Roger.
    "Who does it want to marry?" asked Drew.
    "Its childhood tweetheart."

"What kinds of birds are the best protectors?" asked the teacher.

"The knightingale and the knight owl," answered the student.

^^^^^^^^^^^^^^^^^^^^^^^^^^^^^^^^^^^

Why were the birds punished?
For using fowl language.

BROTHERS & SISTERS

"We're playing school,"
said sis. "Wanna join us?"
"Sure," said brother.
"I'm out sick today."

^^^^^^^^^^^^^^^^^^^^^^^^^^^^^^

Dad: "Where are your ice skates?"
Laurence: "I let sister use them."
Dad: "That was very nice of you. Where is she now?"
Laurence: "She's out on the lake, checking to see if the ice is thick enough."

"Why is little sister crying?" Mom called down the hallway.

"She tried to go downstairs without walking," big sister answered.

∧∧∧∧∧∧∧∧∧∧∧∧∧∧∧∧∧∧∧∧∧∧∧∧∧∧∧∧

Kristin: "Why can't your sister Linda come out and play with us?"
Andie: "She has phonesia."
Kristin: "What in the world is phonesia?"
Andie: "She's being punished for tying up the phone all night long."

∧∧∧∧∧∧∧∧∧∧∧∧∧∧∧∧∧∧∧∧∧∧∧∧∧∧∧∧

"I couldn't sleep last night," said brother.

"Why not?" asked sister.

"I had this dream that the sun had disappeared and wasn't coming back."

"That's ridiculous. You lay awake all night worrying about that?"

"Yeah. Then finally, just a little while ago, it dawned on me. . . ."

"My parents just got a new computer for my teenage sister," said Jon.

"I wish my parents could make that kind of trade for my big sister," said Ron.

∧∧∧∧∧∧∧∧∧∧∧∧∧∧∧∧∧∧∧∧∧∧∧∧∧∧∧∧

"Mom, I want a pet skunk," said Tricia.

"And where, exactly, do you propose to keep it?"

"In brother's room."

"What would he do about the terrible odor?"

"I'm sure the skunk's used to it."

∧∧∧∧∧∧∧∧∧∧∧∧∧∧∧∧∧∧∧∧∧∧∧∧∧∧∧∧

"I really am brilliant," boasted Wylie.

"Prove it," said his brother Bing.

"See that picture puzzle on the table? I finished it all by myself in just three weeks."

"What's so great about that?"

"The box says five to seven years."

"Dad, I'm tired of sleepwalking," said Caleb. "What can I do?"

"Well, let's put your tricycle in your bedroom."

^^^^^^^^^^^^^^^^^^^^^^^^^^^^^^^

"Mom, we think you're fantastic," said Jan. "You're so understanding, and loving, and caring, and organized, and well-dressed—and the greatest cook in America."

"Yeah," agreed Kathy. "We're planning to build you a mom-ument!

^^^^^^^^^^^^^^^^^^^^^^^^^^^^^^^

"What's this?" asked brother.

"It's dessert. I made it," said sister.

"What do you call it?"

"That's pound cake, silly!"

"Oh. I can see why."

"What do you mean?"

"I'll need a hammer to pound out the lumps."

"You must share your cookies with your little brother," Mother scolded Suella. "Why, even chickens and sparrows know the importance of sharing food."

"If we were talking about worms," Suella said, "there would be *no problem*!"

∧∧∧∧∧∧∧∧∧∧∧∧∧∧∧∧∧∧∧∧∧∧∧∧∧∧∧∧∧

"*Oooo!* This wind is terrible," said sis. "It's made a total mess of my hair."

"Yeah," agreed brother. "You look like you've been through a haircane."

∧∧∧∧∧∧∧∧∧∧∧∧∧∧∧∧∧∧∧∧∧∧∧∧∧∧∧∧∧

"Who is your brother?" asked the new minister.

"No, Who is not my brother," corrected Misty. "My brother's name is Patrick."

∧∧∧∧∧∧∧∧∧∧∧∧∧∧∧∧∧∧∧∧∧∧∧∧∧∧∧∧∧

Dee: "I've made the tuna casserole."
Dum: "Good. I thought it was for us."

Dee: "This ointment makes my leg smart."
Dum: "Well, why not rub some on your
head?"

∧∧∧∧∧∧∧∧∧∧∧∧∧∧∧∧∧∧∧∧∧∧∧∧∧∧∧∧

Dee: "Who gave you that black eye?"
Dum: "Nobody. I had to fight for it!"

TONGUE TWISTER

Sue sued Sukie for Sukie's new blue shoes.
Sukie sued Sue for Sue's gooey blue glue.
If Sue sued Sukie and Sukie sued Sue,
Who has the new gooey glued blue shoes?

CATS

"Dad's mad at the cat," said Kristin.

"What did the cat do now?" asked John.

"Dad discovered she's been driving the car at night."

^^^^^^^^^^^^^^^^^^^^^^^^^^^^^

Why couldn't the cat slip through the eye of a needle?
Someone tied a knot in its tail.

^^^^^^^^^^^^^^^^^^^^^^^^^^^^^

"What is your cat's favorite food?" asked David.

"Mice cream," said Micah.

What do you call the grandfather of a
    kitten?
a grandpaw.

∧∧∧∧∧∧∧∧∧∧∧∧∧∧∧∧∧∧∧∧∧∧∧∧∧∧∧∧∧

How did the kitten get to the top of the
    tree?
*It stood on an acorn and waited for it to
    grow.*

∧∧∧∧∧∧∧∧∧∧∧∧∧∧∧∧∧∧∧∧∧∧∧∧∧∧∧∧∧

"Jack, put out the cat," Mother instructed as
the family got ready for bed.
    "I can't, Mom."
    "Why not?"
    "Because it hasn't come in all day."

CHICKENS, TURKEYS, ETC.

How do young chicks escape from their eggs?
Through the eggs-its.

^^^^^^^^^^^^^^^^^^^^^^^^^^^^^

If chickens never really fly, why do they
  have wings?
So we can distinguish them from horses.

^^^^^^^^^^^^^^^^^^^^^^^^^^^^^

What do chickens have to be thankful for on
  Thanksgiving Day?
The fact that they're not turkeys.

Why did the turkey cross the road?
It saw the Pilgrims sailing in.

∧∧∧∧∧∧∧∧∧∧∧∧∧∧∧∧∧∧∧∧∧∧∧∧∧∧∧∧

Why did the Easter bunny cross the road?
To escape the angry children who couldn't find all the hidden eggs.

∧∧∧∧∧∧∧∧∧∧∧∧∧∧∧∧∧∧∧∧∧∧∧∧∧∧∧∧

What do chickens do at Kentucky Fried Chicken?
They kick the bucket.

∧∧∧∧∧∧∧∧∧∧∧∧∧∧∧∧∧∧∧∧∧∧∧∧∧∧∧∧

Why did the kangaroo decide not to cross the road?
It didn't want to be called a chicken.

∧∧∧∧∧∧∧∧∧∧∧∧∧∧∧∧∧∧∧∧∧∧∧∧∧∧∧∧

Why did the chicken cross the playground?
To get to the other slide.

TONGUE TWISTER

If rustlers wrestle wrestlers
While rustlers rustle rustlers,
Could rustlers rustle wrestlers
While wrestlers wrestle rustlers?

COMPUTERS

How did the computer
criminal get out of jail?
Pressed the <Escape> key.

^^^^^^^^^^^^^^^

What is the favorite snack
of computer programmers?
Chips.

^^^^^^^^^^^^^^^

"Did you hear about the spider that enrolled in computer courses?"
"Yeah. It wanted to learn to design Web pages."

What does the baby computer call its daddy?
Da-ta.

^^^^^^^^^^^^^^^^^^^^^^^^^^^^

What's an astronaut's favorite part of a computer?
The spacebar.

^^^^^^^^^^^^^^^^^^^^^^^^^^^^

Why did the computer get up and leave the office?
To go have a byte of lunch.

^^^^^^^^^^^^^^^^^^^^^^^^^^^^

Teacher: "Who was the first American president to use a computer?"
Student: "Warren G. Hard Drive."

^^^^^^^^^^^^^^^^^^^^^^^^^^^^

Why did the computer die?
It had a terminal illness.

"Did you hear about the computer that went to the doctor complaining of a chronic cough?"

"No. What was the diagnosis?"

"It had come down with a virus."

∧∧∧∧∧∧∧∧∧∧∧∧∧∧∧∧∧∧∧∧∧∧∧∧∧∧∧∧

How do you catch computer hackers?
With mousetraps.

∧∧∧∧∧∧∧∧∧∧∧∧∧∧∧∧∧∧∧∧∧∧∧∧∧∧∧∧

What kind of computers wear shades?
The ones that have Windows.

∧∧∧∧∧∧∧∧∧∧∧∧∧∧∧∧∧∧∧∧∧∧∧∧∧∧∧∧

What devices do White House officials use to navigate with computers?
White mice.

∧∧∧∧∧∧∧∧∧∧∧∧∧∧∧∧∧∧∧∧∧∧∧∧∧∧∧∧

How are computers like soldiers?
They all have to boot up.

How do computer spiders catch computer bugs?
They trap them on the World Wide Web.

^^^^^^^^^^^^^^^^^^^^^^^^^^^^^^^^^^

Where do the really cool mice hang out?
In mousepads.

^^^^^^^^^^^^^^^^^^^^^^^^^^^^^^^^^^

What do you call two Internet users who get married?
newlywebs.

^^^^^^^^^^^^^^^^^^^^^^^^^^^^^^^^^^

What did the computer programmers have for a little snack?
Microchips.

COPS & ROBBERS

What do you call a police detective who solves computer crimes?

A hacker tracker.

^^^^^^^^^^^^^^^^^^^^^^^^^^^^^^^^^^

"I think we should rob the Blackstones' house tomorrow night while they're out of town," one burglar said to his partner.

"You're crazy," said the partner. "They must have half a dozen dogs. The barking will wake up the whole neighborhood."

"Nah, I have it figured differently. The dogs will be barking so loudly, nobody will hear us break the window."

"What are you in for?" one prison inmate asked another.

"Robbed a grocery store."

"How much did you get?"

"About $1,500."

"How'd you get caught?"

"Couldn't get away fast enough."

"Why not?"

"The money bags were too heavy. It was all in nickels and pennies."

∧∧∧∧∧∧∧∧∧∧∧∧∧∧∧∧∧∧∧∧∧∧∧∧∧∧∧∧∧∧

Why was the butcher arrested?
The police caught him chop-lifting.

TONGUE TWISTER

Busby burned bananas and bandannas.
Bandannas and bananas Busby burned.

COWS

How can you guarantee milk won't go sour?
Don't milk the cow.

Why did the cow cross the road?
To see what was on the udder side.

What animal says "oom"?
A backward cow.

What do you call a cow eating grass in your yard?
A lawn moo-er.

"If a cow's head is pointed west, in which direction is its tail pointed?" Wade asked.

"East," said Wyatt.

"No," said Wade. "It's pointed down."

∧∧∧∧∧∧∧∧∧∧∧∧∧∧∧∧∧∧∧∧∧∧∧∧∧∧∧∧∧

"I understand your bull wins first prize at the state fair each year," a stranger said to farmer Jackson.

"That's right," said the farmer.

"What do you figure that bull's worth?" asked the stranger.

"Depends."

"What do you mean?"

"Depends on whether you wanna buy him or tax me for him."

∧∧∧∧∧∧∧∧∧∧∧∧∧∧∧∧∧∧∧∧∧∧∧∧∧∧∧∧∧

What do you hear when cows start singing?
Moo-sic.

DEFINITIONS

ant: *an industrious insect that works hardest when it's at a picnic.*

^^^^^^^^^^^^^^^^^^^^^^^^^^^^^^

arcade: *what everyone on Noah's ark drank.*

^^^^^^^^^^^^^^^^^^^^^^^^^^^^^^

bagel: *a gull that prefers the bay to the sea.*

^^^^^^^^^^^^^^^^^^^^^^^^^^^^^^

blooming idiots: *flowers that are stupid in springtime.*

^^^^^^^^^^^^^^^^^^^^^^^^^^^^^^

bookworm: *a highly educated worm.*

board of education: *the school principal's paddle.*

∧∧∧∧∧∧∧∧∧∧∧∧∧∧∧∧∧∧∧∧∧∧∧∧∧∧∧∧

brainstorm: *Albert Einstein being struck on the head by lightning.*

∧∧∧∧∧∧∧∧∧∧∧∧∧∧∧∧∧∧∧∧∧∧∧∧∧∧∧∧

budget: *something that's impossible for an eight-year-old to do with a thousand-pound rock.*

∧∧∧∧∧∧∧∧∧∧∧∧∧∧∧∧∧∧∧∧∧∧∧∧∧∧∧∧

butter: *an aggressive billy goat.*

∧∧∧∧∧∧∧∧∧∧∧∧∧∧∧∧∧∧∧∧∧∧∧∧∧∧∧∧

candlemaker: *someone who works wick ends.*

∧∧∧∧∧∧∧∧∧∧∧∧∧∧∧∧∧∧∧∧∧∧∧∧∧∧∧∧

canteen: *a thirst-aid container.*

∧∧∧∧∧∧∧∧∧∧∧∧∧∧∧∧∧∧∧∧∧∧∧∧∧∧∧∧

cobwebs: *what you find if you don't use the World Wide Web for a few days.*

coronet: *the coroner's daughter.*

^^^^^^^^^^^^^^^^^^^^^^^^^^^^

cross-examination: *a pop quiz given by a mean teacher.*

^^^^^^^^^^^^^^^^^^^^^^^^^^^^

debate: *what you stick on a hook to attract de fish.*

^^^^^^^^^^^^^^^^^^^^^^^^^^^^

decayed: *a period of ten years.*

^^^^^^^^^^^^^^^^^^^^^^^^^^^^

deer antler: *opposite of deer uncler.*

^^^^^^^^^^^^^^^^^^^^^^^^^^^^

dynamite: *a cross between a dinosaur and a termite.*

^^^^^^^^^^^^^^^^^^^^^^^^^^^^

echo: *something grown-ups can't punish for talking back.*

electric bill: *what a duck gets when it runs into a wall socket.*

AAAAAAAAAAAAAAAAAAAAAAAAAAAAA

electrician: *someone who's always wiring for more money.*

AAAAAAAAAAAAAAAAAAAAAAAAAAAAA

enchilada: *an inch-long lada.*

AAAAAAAAAAAAAAAAAAAAAAAAAAAAA

evergreen: *opposite of nevergreen.*

AAAAAAAAAAAAAAAAAAAAAAAAAAAAA

farm: *a place where you work from daybreak 'til backbreak.*

AAAAAAAAAAAAAAAAAAAAAAAAAAAAA

fjord: *a kind of automobile in Norway.*

AAAAAAAAAAAAAAAAAAAAAAAAAAAAA

flashlight: *a plastic or metal container for dead batteries.*

flower: *something that achieves great success by staying in beds.*

∧∧∧∧∧∧∧∧∧∧∧∧∧∧∧∧∧∧∧∧∧∧∧∧∧∧∧∧

flyswatter: *a device that grows at the end of cows.*

∧∧∧∧∧∧∧∧∧∧∧∧∧∧∧∧∧∧∧∧∧∧∧∧∧∧∧∧

friend: *someone who knows everything about you but likes you anyway.*

∧∧∧∧∧∧∧∧∧∧∧∧∧∧∧∧∧∧∧∧∧∧∧∧∧∧∧∧

goose: *a fowl that has to grow up in order to grow down.*

∧∧∧∧∧∧∧∧∧∧∧∧∧∧∧∧∧∧∧∧∧∧∧∧∧∧∧∧

grandfather clock: *an old timer.*

∧∧∧∧∧∧∧∧∧∧∧∧∧∧∧∧∧∧∧∧∧∧∧∧∧∧∧∧

Greece: *a substance used for frying food.*

ground beef: *cattle that graze on grass—as opposed to water beef.*

hardships: *the way the Pilgrims came to America.*

headlines: *marks left by corduroy pillows.*

historian: *someone who just can't let the past lie.*

holiday: *when a famous person has a birthday and they close the schools!*

horse: *an oats-mobile.*

icicles: *the way snowmen travel.*

indigestion: *what happens when a square meal is too large to fit into an oval stomach.*

∧∧∧∧∧∧∧∧∧∧∧∧∧∧∧∧∧∧∧∧∧∧∧∧∧∧∧

infinity: *the place where two parallel lines never meet.*

∧∧∧∧∧∧∧∧∧∧∧∧∧∧∧∧∧∧∧∧∧∧∧∧∧∧∧

jail: *a key club.*

∧∧∧∧∧∧∧∧∧∧∧∧∧∧∧∧∧∧∧∧∧∧∧∧∧∧∧

jet-setter: *a breed of dog that can fly 600 miles an hour at 30,000 feet.*

∧∧∧∧∧∧∧∧∧∧∧∧∧∧∧∧∧∧∧∧∧∧∧∧∧∧∧

kneecap: *a hat for covering your knee.*

∧∧∧∧∧∧∧∧∧∧∧∧∧∧∧∧∧∧∧∧∧∧∧∧∧∧∧

lap: *the part of you that never stands up.*

∧∧∧∧∧∧∧∧∧∧∧∧∧∧∧∧∧∧∧∧∧∧∧∧∧∧∧

leopard: *the animal that's easiest to spot.*

light snack: *a candy-coated candle.*

maneuver: *what farmers put on early crops to help them grow.*

medieval: *the period in history when every-body was half bad.*

misfortune: *daughter of Mr. and Mrs. Fortune.*

mixed emotions: *the kind of feeling you get when your mom comes to get you out of school early in order to take you to the dentist.*

moonlight: *nighttime sunlight.*

∧∧∧∧∧∧∧∧∧∧∧∧∧∧∧∧∧∧∧∧∧∧∧∧∧∧∧∧∧

moth: *husband of a myth.*

∧∧∧∧∧∧∧∧∧∧∧∧∧∧∧∧∧∧∧∧∧∧∧∧∧∧∧∧∧

mountain climber: *an athlete with the gift of grab.*

∧∧∧∧∧∧∧∧∧∧∧∧∧∧∧∧∧∧∧∧∧∧∧∧∧∧∧∧∧

net income: *what a fisherman gets paid.*

∧∧∧∧∧∧∧∧∧∧∧∧∧∧∧∧∧∧∧∧∧∧∧∧∧∧∧∧∧

nightmare: *a horse that prefers to roam at night.*

∧∧∧∧∧∧∧∧∧∧∧∧∧∧∧∧∧∧∧∧∧∧∧∧∧∧∧∧∧

"Nutcracker Suite": *where The Chipmunks stay when they're on tour.*

∧∧∧∧∧∧∧∧∧∧∧∧∧∧∧∧∧∧∧∧∧∧∧∧∧∧∧∧∧

pendulum: *the swingingest part of a clock.*

penguin: *the animal that always wears a tux-edo.*

^^^^^^^^^^^^^^^^^^^^^^^^^^^^^

petrified wood: *a frightened log.*

^^^^^^^^^^^^^^^^^^^^^^^^^^^^^

pharmacy: *where people learn how to pharm.*

^^^^^^^^^^^^^^^^^^^^^^^^^^^^^

pimple: *opposite of dimple.*

^^^^^^^^^^^^^^^^^^^^^^^^^^^^^

popcorn: *father of childcorn.*

^^^^^^^^^^^^^^^^^^^^^^^^^^^^^

prizefight: *a squabble over a Cracker Jacks box.*

^^^^^^^^^^^^^^^^^^^^^^^^^^^^^

professional golfer: *a person who earns a living by playing a round.*

revolving door: *where strangers often meet and go around together.*

∧∧∧∧∧∧∧∧∧∧∧∧∧∧∧∧∧∧∧∧∧∧∧∧∧∧∧∧

riverbank: *where tadpoles save their money.*

∧∧∧∧∧∧∧∧∧∧∧∧∧∧∧∧∧∧∧∧∧∧∧∧∧∧∧∧

rubber band: *musical bicycle tires.*

∧∧∧∧∧∧∧∧∧∧∧∧∧∧∧∧∧∧∧∧∧∧∧∧∧∧∧∧

rustler: *a thief looking for beef.*

∧∧∧∧∧∧∧∧∧∧∧∧∧∧∧∧∧∧∧∧∧∧∧∧∧∧∧∧

skeleton: *a body with the inside out and the outside missing.*

∧∧∧∧∧∧∧∧∧∧∧∧∧∧∧∧∧∧∧∧∧∧∧∧∧∧∧∧

sleet: *precipitation that can't decide whether it wants to be rain or snow.*

∧∧∧∧∧∧∧∧∧∧∧∧∧∧∧∧∧∧∧∧∧∧∧∧∧∧∧∧

smile: *a curve that can straighten out a lot of problems.*

snowball: *where snowmen and snowwomen dance.*

∧∧∧∧∧∧∧∧∧∧∧∧∧∧∧∧∧∧∧∧∧∧∧∧∧∧∧

square: *a circle with corners.*

∧∧∧∧∧∧∧∧∧∧∧∧∧∧∧∧∧∧∧∧∧∧∧∧∧∧∧

steel wool: *what sheep thieves do.*

∧∧∧∧∧∧∧∧∧∧∧∧∧∧∧∧∧∧∧∧∧∧∧∧∧∧∧

stick: *a boomerang that won't return.*

∧∧∧∧∧∧∧∧∧∧∧∧∧∧∧∧∧∧∧∧∧∧∧∧∧∧∧

stock exchange: *the place were cows are traded.*

∧∧∧∧∧∧∧∧∧∧∧∧∧∧∧∧∧∧∧∧∧∧∧∧∧∧∧

stoplight: *opposite of golight.*

∧∧∧∧∧∧∧∧∧∧∧∧∧∧∧∧∧∧∧∧∧∧∧∧∧∧∧

submarine: *a can of people.*

sunspots: *symptoms that the sun has chicken-pox.*

∧∧∧∧∧∧∧∧∧∧∧∧∧∧∧∧∧∧∧∧∧∧∧∧∧∧

sweater: *something you have to put on when Mom gets cold.*

∧∧∧∧∧∧∧∧∧∧∧∧∧∧∧∧∧∧∧∧∧∧∧∧∧∧

sycamore tree: *the sickest tree in the forest.*

∧∧∧∧∧∧∧∧∧∧∧∧∧∧∧∧∧∧∧∧∧∧∧∧∧∧

thumbtacks: *a tax imposed on hitchhikers.*

∧∧∧∧∧∧∧∧∧∧∧∧∧∧∧∧∧∧∧∧∧∧∧∧∧∧

transparent: *a train's father or mother.*

∧∧∧∧∧∧∧∧∧∧∧∧∧∧∧∧∧∧∧∧∧∧∧∧∧∧

vacuum cleaner: *a broom with a stomach.*

∧∧∧∧∧∧∧∧∧∧∧∧∧∧∧∧∧∧∧∧∧∧∧∧∧∧

vicious circle: *the meanest part of geometry class.*

violinist: *a musician who does nothing but fiddle around.*

∧∧∧∧∧∧∧∧∧∧∧∧∧∧∧∧∧∧∧∧∧∧∧∧∧∧∧∧∧

vitamin: *what you should do when your grandparents ring your doorbell.*

∧∧∧∧∧∧∧∧∧∧∧∧∧∧∧∧∧∧∧∧∧∧∧∧∧∧∧∧∧

volcano: *a mountain with burning indigestion.*

∧∧∧∧∧∧∧∧∧∧∧∧∧∧∧∧∧∧∧∧∧∧∧∧∧∧∧∧∧

waffle: *a pancake with treads.*

∧∧∧∧∧∧∧∧∧∧∧∧∧∧∧∧∧∧∧∧∧∧∧∧∧∧∧∧∧

watchdog: *a dog that can tell time.*

∧∧∧∧∧∧∧∧∧∧∧∧∧∧∧∧∧∧∧∧∧∧∧∧∧∧∧∧∧

webbing: *the happy occasion when spiders get married.*

∧∧∧∧∧∧∧∧∧∧∧∧∧∧∧∧∧∧∧∧∧∧∧∧∧∧∧∧∧

wig: *a convertible top.*

wombat: *what you use to strike at a womball.*

∧∧∧∧∧∧∧∧∧∧∧∧∧∧∧∧∧∧∧∧∧∧∧∧∧∧∧∧∧∧

woodpecker: *the knockingbird.*

∧∧∧∧∧∧∧∧∧∧∧∧∧∧∧∧∧∧∧∧∧∧∧∧∧∧∧∧∧∧

yardstick: *something that has a third foot but still can't crawl, walk, or run.*

∧∧∧∧∧∧∧∧∧∧∧∧∧∧∧∧∧∧∧∧∧∧∧∧∧∧∧∧∧∧

zoo: *a jail for animals.*

TONGUE TWISTER

Sliver hither, Zither!

Sneaky thieves seized the skis.

THE DOCTOR

"My son says he feels like an apple," Mother told the doctor. "I don't understand what's wrong with him."

"Well, bring him on in for a check-up," said the doctor. "I won't bite him."

~~~~~~~~~~~~~~~~~~~~~~~~~~~~~~~

"Doc, I need a prescription."

"For yourself?"

"No, it's for my fireplace."

"Your fireplace? What seems to be the trouble?"

"I think it has the flue."

What did the elevator say to the doctor?
"I'm coming down with something."

∧∧∧∧∧∧∧∧∧∧∧∧∧∧∧∧∧∧∧∧∧∧∧∧∧∧∧∧

Dental patient: "How much would you charge to pull that bad tooth of mine?"
Dentist: "Our regular rate for pulling teeth: $75."
Patient: "Well, how much would you charge to loosen it for me?"

∧∧∧∧∧∧∧∧∧∧∧∧∧∧∧∧∧∧∧∧∧∧∧∧∧∧∧∧

"Doctor, I think I'm sick," said the alligator.
"That makes you an illigator," said the doctor.

∧∧∧∧∧∧∧∧∧∧∧∧∧∧∧∧∧∧∧∧∧∧∧∧∧∧∧∧

"Doctor," screamed a caller on the phone, "I've just swallowed a camera with a roll of film in it."
"Well, just sit tight," the doctor said. "Let's wait and see what develops."

Patient: "What do you want?"
Nurse: "I came to take your blood pressure."
Patient: "I need it. Use your own blood pressure."

∧∧∧∧∧∧∧∧∧∧∧∧∧∧∧∧∧∧∧∧∧∧∧∧∧∧∧∧∧

Why did the window have to be taken to the doctor's office?
It was suffering from windowpanes.

∧∧∧∧∧∧∧∧∧∧∧∧∧∧∧∧∧∧∧∧∧∧∧∧∧∧∧∧∧

Why did the stand-up comic go see the doctor?
She had tired feet.

∧∧∧∧∧∧∧∧∧∧∧∧∧∧∧∧∧∧∧∧∧∧∧∧∧∧∧∧∧

How can a surgeon tell whether a patient is a librarian or an electrician?
The heart, lungs, liver, kidneys, and stomach of a librarian are all numbered. The insides of an electrician are color-coded.

"Doctor, my tooth is loose."
"Try gluing it with toothpaste."

^^^^^^^^^^^^^^^^^^^^^^^^^^^^^^^

"How can I stop this nosebleed?" a patient asked.

"Hold your breath until your heart stops beating," said the doctor.

^^^^^^^^^^^^^^^^^^^^^^^^^^^^^^^

"Well, I believe we've solved your little hearing problem with these hearing aids," the doctor said. "That will be $900."

The patient pretended not to hear, and walked out the door.

^^^^^^^^^^^^^^^^^^^^^^^^^^^^^^^

"My neck hurts every time I turn my head," complained the patient. "What should I do?"

"Don't turn your head," recommended the doctor.

The doctor was trying to cheer Artie, who'd sprained his wrist. "When you get out of this sling," the doctor told him, "you'll feel better than ever. You'll be able to write, catch Frisbees, and bounce basketballs with the best of them."

Artie stopped crying and brightened up. "Wow!" he said. "I've never been able to bounce a basketball before!"

∧∧∧∧∧∧∧∧∧∧∧∧∧∧∧∧∧∧∧∧∧∧∧∧∧∧∧∧

"How do you feel?" asked the doctor.
   "Like a dog," moaned Katie.
   "Well, sit," the doctor said. "Stay."

∧∧∧∧∧∧∧∧∧∧∧∧∧∧∧∧∧∧∧∧∧∧∧∧∧∧∧∧

"Doc, there's something wrong with my soda crackers."
   "What are the symptoms?"
   "They feel crumby."

"Doctor, my ear won't stop ringing."
"Then answer it."

TONGUE TWISTER

Chip chopped chuck
for chipped chuck soup.
Chipped chuck soup was
chopped by Chip.

DOGS

"Mom, the dog bit sister's hand again!"

"Uh-oh. We'd better take a look. We may need to put something on it."

"Nah, I think the dog prefers her hand plain."

∧∧∧∧∧∧∧∧∧∧∧∧∧∧∧∧∧∧∧∧∧∧∧∧∧∧∧

Why did the dog refuse to wear its wrist watch?
Because the watch had ticks.

∧∧∧∧∧∧∧∧∧∧∧∧∧∧∧∧∧∧∧∧∧∧∧∧∧∧∧

At what point in history were dogs happiest?
During the Bone Age.

Myra: "Our dog must be older than we thought."
Luke: "What makes you think so?"
Myra: "She's started bringing in yesterday's newspaper."

∧∧∧∧∧∧∧∧∧∧∧∧∧∧∧∧∧∧∧∧∧∧∧∧∧∧∧∧∧

"We had to buy our dog a longer leash," Zan said.
   "Why?" asked Van.
   "Dad kept stepping on its tail."

∧∧∧∧∧∧∧∧∧∧∧∧∧∧∧∧∧∧∧∧∧∧∧∧∧∧∧∧∧

"What do you think of my police dog?"
   "Dog? That animal says 'meoww'!"
   "Yes. It's working undercover at the moment."

∧∧∧∧∧∧∧∧∧∧∧∧∧∧∧∧∧∧∧∧∧∧∧∧∧∧∧∧∧

What sign did the bulldog put in front of its doghouse?
Beware of Resident

"What's your dog's name?"

"Ginger, when she's not biting people."

"What's her name when she *is* biting people?"

"Ginger Snaps."

∧∧∧∧∧∧∧∧∧∧∧∧∧∧∧∧∧∧∧∧∧∧∧∧∧

"Do you think Dottie's clean?" asked Myra, bringing her Dalmatian to show Mom after bathing the dog.

"Yes," Mom said, inspecting the ears and paws. "She's pretty clean."

"Actually," said Myra, "I think she's pretty even when she's dirty."

∧∧∧∧∧∧∧∧∧∧∧∧∧∧∧∧∧∧∧∧∧∧∧∧∧

What do you call a nature film about dogs? *Dog-umentaries.*

∧∧∧∧∧∧∧∧∧∧∧∧∧∧∧∧∧∧∧∧∧∧∧∧∧

Who do dogs mail their Christmas wish lists to? *Santa Paws.*

"If you were being chased by two German shepherds," posed Erin, "what steps would you take?"

"Long ones," said Bart.

^^^^^^^^^^^^^^^^^^^^^^^^^^^^^

"Does your dog Dolly have fleas?" asked Brianne.

"No—but she just had puppies!" said Erica.

^^^^^^^^^^^^^^^^^^^^^^^^^^^^^

What do you call it when two dogs negotiate?
Flea bargaining.

^^^^^^^^^^^^^^^^^^^^^^^^^^^^^

"My dog knows how to wash my clothes for me," said Chip.

"Is that what you call a 'laundromutt'?" asked Trip.

The Johnstons invited their new neighbors the Andersons for dinner. Everyone was having a great time, enjoying the food and conversation. Mr. Anderson was curious, though, to observe that the Johnstons' dog sat right beside him on the floor and stared at him the whole evening.

"This is a very nice dog you have," Mr. Anderson said. "But I wonder why he keeps looking at me like that."

"Probably," the Johnstons' little boy suggested, "it's because you're eating off of his plate."

A movie screenwriter waited eagerly for word on whether her latest work had been accepted by any of the film companies. She hounded her agent every day. Finally, the agent phoned her to report.

"Good news," the agent said. "Warner Brothers loved your script and literally ate it up."

"That's wonderful!" beamed the screenwriter. "So when will they be making the movie?"

"Well, there's one small problem. Warner Brothers is my dog. . . ."

TONGUE TWISTER

Eight bright lights.
Great bright nights.

ELEPHANTS

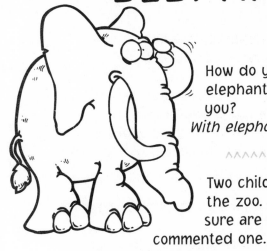

How do you stop an elephant from chasing you?
With elephant repellent.

Two children were at the zoo. "Elephants sure are fat animals," commented one.

"Yeah. I guess my mom was right when she said peanuts are fattening."

What kind of vegetable do you find under elephants' feet?
Squash.

How does an elephant get down a chimney?
It volunteers as one of Santa's helpers and hides in the toy sack.

∧∧∧∧∧∧∧∧∧∧∧∧∧∧∧∧∧∧∧∧∧∧∧∧∧∧∧∧

Why do most elephants look fat?
They go to inexperienced tailors.

∧∧∧∧∧∧∧∧∧∧∧∧∧∧∧∧∧∧∧∧∧∧∧∧∧∧∧∧

How do you trap an elephant?
Take a big net, hide in the jungle, and sound like a peanut.

∧∧∧∧∧∧∧∧∧∧∧∧∧∧∧∧∧∧∧∧∧∧∧∧∧∧∧∧

What's huge, gray, has a trunk, and goes up and down?
An elephant on an elevator.

∧∧∧∧∧∧∧∧∧∧∧∧∧∧∧∧∧∧∧∧∧∧∧∧∧∧∧∧

What wears beautiful slippers and weighs several tons?
Cinderelephant.

What do you get when you cross an elephant
with an overloaded computer?
A crash through the jungle.

∧∧∧∧∧∧∧∧∧∧∧∧∧∧∧∧∧∧∧∧∧∧∧∧∧∧∧∧

If an elephant falls into a cup of coffee,
what's the result?
*Death by drowning. Elephants don't swim well
in coffee.*

∧∧∧∧∧∧∧∧∧∧∧∧∧∧∧∧∧∧∧∧∧∧∧∧∧∧∧∧

What's gray and red, weighs 4,000 pounds,
and has two trunks and eight legs?
Two elephants wearing red bikinis.

∧∧∧∧∧∧∧∧∧∧∧∧∧∧∧∧∧∧∧∧∧∧∧∧∧∧∧∧

William: "I can stop a charging elephant with
one hand."
Pete: "I don't believe an elephant with one
hand would be charging."

What did the elephants wear at the swimming pool?
Trunks.

^^^^^^^^^^^^^^^^^^^^^^^^^^^^^^^^^^^

Teacher: "Which is taller—an elephant or a giraffe?"
Student: "They're both the same height."
Teacher: "You're forgetting that the giraffe has that very long neck. That means when it raises its head, it has greater height."
Student: "Yes, but their feet all go to the exact same depth."

FAMOUS CHARACTERS

Who loves to solve mysteries and soak in bubble baths?
Sherlock Foams.

∧∧∧∧∧∧∧∧∧∧∧∧∧∧∧∧∧

Mike: "What do you do for a living?"
Harve: "I get fired every day."
Mike: "How can you earn a living by getting fired every day?"
Harve: "I'm the star of the circus. I'm the guy they call the Human Cannonball."

Humpty Dumpty sat on a wall.
  Humpty Dumpty had a great fall. . .
but winter wasn't much to speak of.

∧∧∧∧∧∧∧∧∧∧∧∧∧∧∧∧∧∧∧∧∧∧∧∧∧∧∧

Teacher: "What is Abraham Lincoln most
    famous for?"
Student: "The $5 bill."

∧∧∧∧∧∧∧∧∧∧∧∧∧∧∧∧∧∧∧∧∧∧∧∧∧∧∧

Brit and his family were about to take off on
an airplane.
  "You need to buckle your seatbelt now,"
his dad said.
  "But I'm Superman," Brit complained. "I
don't need to wear a seatbelt."
  "If you were Superman, you wouldn't need
an airplane, either."

∧∧∧∧∧∧∧∧∧∧∧∧∧∧∧∧∧∧∧∧∧∧∧∧∧∧∧

What do you call Batman after he's been
    flattened by a steamroller?
Flatman.

Who makes a sound like "ninety-nine-THUMP,
    ninety-nine-THUMP" when he walks?
Long John Centipede.

∧∧∧∧∧∧∧∧∧∧∧∧∧∧∧∧∧∧∧∧∧∧∧∧∧∧∧∧∧

"Did you hear about Vincent van Gogh's
cousin who started the stagecoach line?"
    "No. What was his name?"
    "Wells Far Gogh."

∧∧∧∧∧∧∧∧∧∧∧∧∧∧∧∧∧∧∧∧∧∧∧∧∧∧∧∧∧

"Did you hear about van Gogh's other cousin
who was a famous lady magician?"
    "No. What was her name?"
    "Where Didshe Gogh."

FARM LIFE

Alvin: "Wow, that scarecrow sure is scary!"

Marvin: "Yeah, I bet the birds are so scared they bring back the food they took last year."

∧∧∧∧∧∧∧∧∧∧∧∧∧∧∧∧∧∧∧∧∧∧∧∧∧∧∧

What's a lamb's favorite meat sauce?
Baa-baa-que sauce.

∧∧∧∧∧∧∧∧∧∧∧∧∧∧∧∧∧∧∧∧∧∧∧∧∧∧∧

Where do gardeners mail their letters?
At the nearest U.S. Compost Office.

"Do you think we should buy a horse or a cow with our harvest money this autumn?" a farmer asked his wife.

"Well, the neighbors sure would laugh at you if they saw you trying to milk a horse."

"That's true. Of course, they'd laugh at me if they saw me trying to ride a cow, too."

∧∧∧∧∧∧∧∧∧∧∧∧∧∧∧∧∧∧∧∧∧∧∧∧∧∧∧∧

Why should you never tell a secret in a corn-field?
Because the stalks have ears.

∧∧∧∧∧∧∧∧∧∧∧∧∧∧∧∧∧∧∧∧∧∧∧∧∧∧∧∧

What did the farmer do when he finally caught the stray pig?
Put it in hamcuffs.

∧∧∧∧∧∧∧∧∧∧∧∧∧∧∧∧∧∧∧∧∧∧∧∧∧∧∧∧

Why was the farmer so stressed out?
He was studying for the soil test.

"Daddy, what will we do with the hog after we butcher it?" asked the farm lad.

"Then we cure the meat."

The boy scratched his head. "Don't we have things backward, Daddy?"

"What do you mean, son?"

"Well, it seems to me that if we're gonna try to cure it, we should do that while the hog's still alive."

∧∧∧∧∧∧∧∧∧∧∧∧∧∧∧∧∧∧∧∧∧∧∧∧∧∧∧

"What's the name of your hog?"

"Ballpoint."

"Why do you call it Ballpoint?"

"Actually, that's just its pen name."

∧∧∧∧∧∧∧∧∧∧∧∧∧∧∧∧∧∧∧∧∧∧∧∧∧∧∧

"My dad grows corn so big he gets three dollars an ear at market," said one farm lad.

"That's nothing," said his friend. "My dad grows cantaloupe so big it takes only three to make a dozen."

"How have you been doing?" asked Farmer Smith.

"Not too well," said Farmer Brown. "I just got out of the hospital."

"Land sakes! What was wrong?"

"I was kicked in the head by my old mule."

"What a terrible accident!"

"Wasn't an accident. I reckon the mule did it on purpose."

∧∧∧∧∧∧∧∧∧∧∧∧∧∧∧∧∧∧∧∧∧∧∧∧∧∧∧∧∧∧

"My farmer cousin just got back from vacation. It was the first time he'd taken a break from farming in more than ten years."

"Where did he go?"

"To the beach."

"Oh, he must have enjoyed that!"

"He sure did. He was a little disappointed with surfing, though. The tractor engine kept choking down in the surf."

What happened when the pig pen broke?
The pig had to start using a pencil.

^^^^^^^^^^^^^^^^^^^^^^^^^^^^

What did the farmer say when he found a
   hole in one of his pumpkins?
"I think I need a pumpkin patch."

^^^^^^^^^^^^^^^^^^^^^^^^^^^^

What's the difference between a granary
   and a grandpa?
One's a corn bin. The other's your born kin.

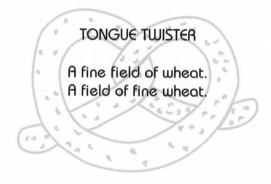

TONGUE TWISTER

A fine field of wheat.
A field of fine wheat.

FISH

Kippie: "I caught a
    fish yesterday
    that weighed ten
    pounds!"
Mickie: "I don't
    believe it."
    Kippie: "It's true. The
picture alone weighed almost a pound."

∧∧∧∧∧∧∧∧∧∧∧∧∧∧∧∧∧∧∧∧∧∧∧∧∧∧∧∧∧

In what country can fish survive out of
    water?
Finland.

∧∧∧∧∧∧∧∧∧∧∧∧∧∧∧∧∧∧∧∧∧∧∧∧∧∧∧∧∧

What's the most famous fish in the world?
The starfish.

"Jerry, I insist that you take your little brother fishing with you," Dad said sternly.

"But Dad, he—"

"No buts. He needs to learn how to fish, and you can teach him while I'm busy here in the shop."

"But Dad, he—"

"I told you, no buts. Now go."

"But there's no bait."

"What do you mean? I just bought you a box of crickets."

"Little brother has already eaten 'em all."

∧∧∧∧∧∧∧∧∧∧∧∧∧∧∧∧∧∧∧∧∧∧∧∧∧∧∧∧∧

What did the fish boat captain say to the card magician?
Pick a cod, any cod.

∧∧∧∧∧∧∧∧∧∧∧∧∧∧∧∧∧∧∧∧∧∧∧∧∧∧∧∧∧

What are the first things fish learn in school?
Their A-B-Seas.

Who are hammerhead sharks' best friends?
Nailhead sharks.

∧∧∧∧∧∧∧∧∧∧∧∧∧∧∧∧∧∧∧∧∧∧∧∧∧∧∧∧∧

"I keep my goldfish in a huge tank," said Mark.
"I keep mine in the bathtub," said Mitch.
"In the bathtub? What do you do with them when you need to take a bath?"
"I make them cover their eyes."

∧∧∧∧∧∧∧∧∧∧∧∧∧∧∧∧∧∧∧∧∧∧∧∧∧∧∧∧∧

"You can't catch fish here," the game warden told Timmy. "You don't have a license."
"Well, I haven't had a bite all day," Timmy said. "I doubt I could catch fish here even if I did have a license."

∧∧∧∧∧∧∧∧∧∧∧∧∧∧∧∧∧∧∧∧∧∧∧∧∧∧∧∧∧

Why do goldfish have to be kept inside?
Because they'll slip through the leash if you try to take them out for a walk.

What are tropical fishes' favorite foods?
Reef-fried beans.

∧∧∧∧∧∧∧∧∧∧∧∧∧∧∧∧∧∧∧∧∧∧∧∧∧∧∧∧

Two boys were walking home from the creek with a nice string of fish. They'd had a great day fishing, but their prizes were starting to emit a strong, unpleasant odor.

"I sure wish there was some way we could keep 'em from smelling," said one boy.

"Well," said the other, "I reckon we could clamp their noses."

∧∧∧∧∧∧∧∧∧∧∧∧∧∧∧∧∧∧∧∧∧∧∧∧∧∧∧∧

How do you catch a school of fish?
With a bookworm.

∧∧∧∧∧∧∧∧∧∧∧∧∧∧∧∧∧∧∧∧∧∧∧∧∧∧∧∧

Blake: "We're not catching any fish. Why don't you tell them to start biting?"
Jake: "How can I communicate with a fish?"
Blake: "Drop them another line."

FOOD

What did one blueberry say to the other?
"You sure got us into a jam this time."

∧∧∧∧∧∧∧∧∧∧∧∧∧∧∧∧∧∧∧∧∧∧∧∧∧∧∧∧

What's the favorite food of astronauts?
Launch meat.

∧∧∧∧∧∧∧∧∧∧∧∧∧∧∧∧∧∧∧∧∧∧∧∧∧∧∧∧

What do you call a lazy butcher?
A meatloafer.

∧∧∧∧∧∧∧∧∧∧∧∧∧∧∧∧∧∧∧∧∧∧∧∧∧∧∧∧

"Where can I get a chicken dinner cheap?"
   "Try the feed store."

What did the strawberry do when it couldn't get a date for the breakfast dance?
It invited a raisin.

^^^^^^^^^^^^^^^^^^^^^^^^^^^^^^

"Mother, that's your third helping of eggs!"
"I love eggs, dear. They're good for you."
"But I'm afraid you're going to turn into a momelette!"

^^^^^^^^^^^^^^^^^^^^^^^^^^^^^^

What becomes of cabbage and carrots if you accidentally store them in the freezer instead of the refrigerator?
They turn into cold slaw.

^^^^^^^^^^^^^^^^^^^^^^^^^^^^^^

"Oooo!" shrieked Clark. "This cheese is dreadful! It has holes in it!"
"Never mind that," his mother said. "Just eat the cheese. You don't have to eat the holes today."

"Breakfast this morning was out of this world," said Mollie.

"What did you have?" teased Dollie. "Flying sausages?"

^^^^^^^^^^^^^^^^^^^^^^^^^^^^^^^^

What did the cake batter say to the spatula?
"Stop stirring at me!"

^^^^^^^^^^^^^^^^^^^^^^^^^^^^^^^^

"How much do you like spinach?"
"Actually, I like nothing better."

^^^^^^^^^^^^^^^^^^^^^^^^^^^^^^^^

What food do you find on the honor roll?
Brilliant butter.

^^^^^^^^^^^^^^^^^^^^^^^^^^^^^^^^

What's the difference between a moldy vegetable and a depressing song?
One is a bad salad, and the other is a sad ballad.

"Oh, no, not fried chicken," moaned little Cindy, coming into the kitchen for dinner. "I don't think I can *stand* to eat fried chicken this evening!"

"Why not?" asked her mother. "You liked it last night and the night before that, and the night before that. . . ."

^^^^^^^^^^^^^^^^^^^^^^^^^^^^^^^^

What's a miner's favorite food?
Coal slaw.

^^^^^^^^^^^^^^^^^^^^^^^^^^^^^^^^

"My mom sure gets mean when she's in the kitchen," Scot said.

"What does she do?" asked Branden.

"She does things like beat the cake mix, mash the potatoes, whip the cream. . ."

^^^^^^^^^^^^^^^^^^^^^^^^^^^^^^^^

What's a puppy's favorite pizza topping?
Pupperoni.

What kind of cheese makes the best building material?
Cottage cheese.

∧∧∧∧∧∧∧∧∧∧∧∧∧∧∧∧∧∧∧∧∧∧∧∧∧∧

What can you always find to eat if you're shipwrecked on a deserted island?
Lots of sand-wiches.

∧∧∧∧∧∧∧∧∧∧∧∧∧∧∧∧∧∧∧∧∧∧∧∧∧∧

What kind of food comes in a can and doesn't make a sound?
Corned-beef hush.

∧∧∧∧∧∧∧∧∧∧∧∧∧∧∧∧∧∧∧∧∧∧∧∧∧∧

What national park is famous for its desserts?
Jellystone.

∧∧∧∧∧∧∧∧∧∧∧∧∧∧∧∧∧∧∧∧∧∧∧∧∧∧

How do you repair a strawberry?
With a strawberry patch.

What made the pickle so sour?
It had a jarring ordeal.

∧∧∧∧∧∧∧∧∧∧∧∧∧∧∧∧∧∧∧∧∧∧∧∧∧∧∧∧∧

What flying machine is good to eat?
The jellycopter.

∧∧∧∧∧∧∧∧∧∧∧∧∧∧∧∧∧∧∧∧∧∧∧∧∧∧∧∧∧

"Where are you going?" one slice of bread asked another.

"I'm going to mail this postcard."

"But bread slices can't mail postcards."

"Sure we can. That's what the toast office is there for."

∧∧∧∧∧∧∧∧∧∧∧∧∧∧∧∧∧∧∧∧∧∧∧∧∧∧∧∧∧

A woman returned to the supermarket with her nine bags of groceries and a long receipt. She demanded to see the store manager.

"What's the problem?" the manager asked.

"You can see right here on the receipt that I paid for two TV dinners," the woman fumed. "So where's the TV?"

TONGUE TWISTER

Does Steve still strew straw
in the still straw stall?

FROGS

How do frogs handle stress?
When something bugs them, they simply eat it.

^^^^^^^^^^^^^^^^^^^^^^^^^^^^^^^^

"My pet frog can work math problems," bragged Buster.

"No way," said Bryce. "Show me."

Buster held his frog in his palm and asked it, "What's ten minus ten?"

And the frog said nothing.

The question on the biology test asked: "Name three kinds of frogs."

The student wrote: "daddy frog, mama frog, baby frog."

∧∧∧∧∧∧∧∧∧∧∧∧∧∧∧∧∧∧∧∧∧∧∧∧∧∧∧

What do you call a nine-foot-high stack of frogs?
A toadem pole.

∧∧∧∧∧∧∧∧∧∧∧∧∧∧∧∧∧∧∧∧∧∧∧∧∧∧∧

What kind of shoes do frogs wear?
Open-toad slippers.

∧∧∧∧∧∧∧∧∧∧∧∧∧∧∧∧∧∧∧∧∧∧∧∧∧∧∧

What's the best way to clear frogs off your car windows?
With the defrogger.

∧∧∧∧∧∧∧∧∧∧∧∧∧∧∧∧∧∧∧∧∧∧∧∧∧∧∧

"Let's go see a movie," suggested one frog to another.

"Okay. I hope it has a hoppy ending."

What do you get when you cross a frog and a chair?
A toadstool.

GROWN-UPS

What did Dad write on the bottom of his shoe?
A footnote.

∧∧∧∧∧∧∧∧∧∧∧∧∧∧∧∧∧∧∧∧∧∧∧∧∧∧∧∧∧∧

"Did you take a shower this morning, son?"
  "No, Mom. Are we missing one?"

∧∧∧∧∧∧∧∧∧∧∧∧∧∧∧∧∧∧∧∧∧∧∧∧∧∧∧∧∧∧

"I reckon I know why parents and grandparents are called 'grown-ups'," said Travis.
  "Why is that?" asked Mavis.
  "Because they're always groaning."

A woman hurried inside a beauty shop mopping her face with a handkerchief. "It must be ninety degrees outside," she told the cosmetologist. "Can you give me some hair-conditioning?"

∧∧∧∧∧∧∧∧∧∧∧∧∧∧∧∧∧∧∧∧∧∧∧∧∧∧∧∧∧∧

"You look so cute when you're asleep," Mother said, tucking Cassie into bed.

"Thanks, Mom, but I wouldn't know," said Cassie.

∧∧∧∧∧∧∧∧∧∧∧∧∧∧∧∧∧∧∧∧∧∧∧∧∧∧∧∧∧∧

Two fathers were discussing their children, who were in college.

"My daughter will graduate next May," said one proudly. "Then she plans to start work as an engineer."

"I'm not sure when my son will graduate," said the other father dejectedly.

"Well, what do expect he'll be when he does graduate?"

"I expect he'll be a senior citizen."

"I'm never going to get married," Belinda announced.

"Why not?" asked her friend.

"I just don't need a husband. I already have a father who snores, a mother who takes out the garbage, and a brother with stinky feet."

^^^^^^^^^^^^^^^^^^^^^^^^^^^^^^^^^^

Mack: "Man, I really was in hot water last night after coming home all muddy from the river."

Zack: "Me, too. My mom made me take a bath."

^^^^^^^^^^^^^^^^^^^^^^^^^^^^^^^^^^

"Mom, may I have a snare drum?"

"Definitely not. Those things are far too loud for the peace and quiet of the neighborhood."

"But Mom, I promise I'll only play it while everyone's asleep."

Dad opened the monthly electric bill and almost fainted when he saw the amount. "This," he groaned, "is what I call a shock!"

^^^^^^^^^^^^^^^^^^^^^^^^^^^^^^^^^^^

Josh: "My dad manages a whole chain of convenience stores."
Mia: "What does a manager do?"
Josh: "Goes around and trains the staff, counts the money, checks the locks to see that everything is secure. Since they're all open twenty-four hours a day, every day of the year, that's a big responsibility."
Mia: "If they're open round the clock. . .why do they have locks?"

^^^^^^^^^^^^^^^^^^^^^^^^^^^^^^^^^^^

"I'm too tired to go to bed, even," Crystal said wearily to her dad.
"Well, you'd better find some energy somewhere," her dad replied. "Your bed's not going to come to you."

"Grandma, how long have you been sewing?"
"Since I was about four years old."
"Wow! If I were you, I'd be bored by now!"

∧∧∧∧∧∧∧∧∧∧∧∧∧∧∧∧∧∧∧∧∧∧∧∧∧∧∧∧

"Oh, dear," Grandmother said as she drove her grandchildren to school. "I just realized I've been speeding for the last several miles."

"Don't worry," piped up Al in the backseat. "The patrol car with the flashing lights behind you is doing the same speed, so it must be all right."

∧∧∧∧∧∧∧∧∧∧∧∧∧∧∧∧∧∧∧∧∧∧∧∧∧∧∧∧

A small child woke up his parents by hollering in the middle of the night.

"What is it?" his dad asked.

"There's a monster under my bed!"

Dad made his way to the closet in the dark. He opened and then slammed the closet door. "There," he said. "I've locked up the monster. Go back to sleep."

"Mom, what month of the year were you married in?"

"June."

"Dad, what month of the year were you married in?"

"June."

"Mom, what day of the week were you married on?"

"It was a Friday evening at seven o'clock."

"Dad, what day of the week were you married on?"

"Friday at seven, same as your mother."

"Wow! Now *that's* what I call a coincidence!"

^^^^^^^^^^^^^^^^^^^^^^^^^^^^

"Mom, I have a stomachache."

"I don't doubt it. You hardly touched your lunch, and you only picked at your dinner. When your stomach is empty, it lets you know by aching."

"So when you complain of a headache, does that mean your head's empty?"

"Mom, Barry just swallowed the remote control to the television set!"

"Well, then, go outside and ride your bikes for a while."

TONGUE TWISTER

The best breath test tests breath better.

Kick six sticks quick.

HISTORY

"Who became famous for inventing the cotton gin?" the teacher asked.

"A guy named Cotton," said the student.

^^^^^^^^^^^^^^^^^^^^^^^^^^^^^^^^

"What can you tell us about the Iron Age?" asked the teacher.

The student thought a moment. "Well, I imagine things got pretty rusty after heavy rains."

^^^^^^^^^^^^^^^^^^^^^^^^^^^^^^^

How did medieval soldiers learn to fight?
They enrolled in knight classes.

Teacher: "What was the cause of the American Revolution?"

Student: "The traffic problem."

Teacher: "Traffic problem? There were no cars, trucks, or buses in those days. There were only horses and wagons."

Student: "But you said a few weeks ago that the colonists started the Revolution because they didn't like the king's taxis."

∧∧∧∧∧∧∧∧∧∧∧∧∧∧∧∧∧∧∧∧∧∧∧∧∧∧∧∧

"What is believed to have happened to the people of the Stone Age?" asked the teacher.

"They were all petrified," said the student.

∧∧∧∧∧∧∧∧∧∧∧∧∧∧∧∧∧∧∧∧∧∧∧∧∧∧∧∧

"Why did the early settlers wear three-cornered hats?" asked the history teacher.

"Because they had three-cornered heads?" Alison suggested.

Teacher: "What year was the Magna Carta signed?"
Student: "I don't know. That was long before I was born."

^^^^^^^^^^^^^^^^^^^^^^^^^^^^^^^^

Where have English kings and queens always been crowned?
On the head.

^^^^^^^^^^^^^^^^^^^^^^^^^^^^^^^^

History teacher: "Why were the Middle Ages called the 'Dark Ages'?"
Student: "Because of all the knights."

^^^^^^^^^^^^^^^^^^^^^^^^^^^^^^^^

"Who were you named after?"
  "George Washington."
  "But your name is Bert."
  "So what? I was named more than two hundred years after they named George Washington."

Student: "Is it true that President Lincoln wrote the Gettysburg Address while riding from Washington to the battleground on the back of an envelope?"

Teacher: "Yes, that's what the history books tell us."

Student: "How many legs did the envelope have?"

ΛΛΛΛΛΛΛΛΛΛΛΛΛΛΛΛΛΛΛΛΛΛΛΛΛΛΛΛΛΛ

Teacher: "Who was John Paul Jones?"

Student: "He was a great American nasal hero."

ΛΛΛΛΛΛΛΛΛΛΛΛΛΛΛΛΛΛΛΛΛΛΛΛΛΛΛΛΛΛ

What did King Henry the Eighth and Popeye the Sailorman have in common?

Same middle name.

ΛΛΛΛΛΛΛΛΛΛΛΛΛΛΛΛΛΛΛΛΛΛΛΛΛΛΛΛΛΛ

"Who's your favorite leader of the Middle Ages?" the teacher asked.

"My daddy!" said little Myra.

HORSES

Which side of a horse usually has the most hair?
The outside.

∧∧∧∧∧∧∧∧∧∧∧∧∧∧∧∧∧∧∧∧

"How's your sick horse?" one rancher asked another.
"She's in stable condition."

∧∧∧∧∧∧∧∧∧∧∧∧∧∧∧∧∧∧∧∧∧∧∧∧∧

"Grandpa, why is it that horses can stand up and walk so much sooner after they're born than humans can?" Neil asked.
"Well, it's partly because they have twice as many legs as humans do, I suppose."

Why did the rancher take the horse to the vet?
The horse had hay fever.

∧∧∧∧∧∧∧∧∧∧∧∧∧∧∧∧∧∧∧∧∧∧∧∧∧∧∧∧∧∧

What kind of horse sees just as well with its tail as with its head?
A horse that's asleep.

∧∧∧∧∧∧∧∧∧∧∧∧∧∧∧∧∧∧∧∧∧∧∧∧∧∧∧∧∧∧

What did one horse say to the other when they ran out of hay?
"Now that's the last straw!"

∧∧∧∧∧∧∧∧∧∧∧∧∧∧∧∧∧∧∧∧∧∧∧∧∧∧∧∧∧∧

Alicia: "Do you know what it means when you find a horseshoe?"
Pat: "Yes. It means some poor horse probably has a sore foot by now."

INSECTS

"What's in style this season?" an insect asked a tailor. "Yellow jackets."

^^^^^^^^^^^^

Maria: "My school class has adopted a talking bird!"

Patsy: "That's nothing. My class has a spelling bee."

^^^^^^^^^^^^^^^^^^^^^^^^^^^^

How do spiders prefer their corn?
On the cobweb.

What kind of surgery is done in grasshopper
    hospitals?
Hoperations.

AAAAAAAAAAAAAAAAAAAAAAAAAAA

What highways do dogs and cats hate most?
Fleaways.

AAAAAAAAAAAAAAAAAAAAAAAAAAA

"It's New Year's Day," said one beetle to
another. "Have you made any resolutions?"
    "Yeah," said the other. "I'm gonna turn
over a new leaf."

AAAAAAAAAAAAAAAAAAAAAAAAAAA

Marie: "I think the ant is just the coolest
    animal! It works all day, effortlessly—
    and do you know how much it can get
    accomplished?"
Matt: "Yeah, a lot—until somebody steps
    on it."

"We have a real problem with biting insects around our yard," a customer told a pharmacist. "What can we do about it?"

"Stop biting them," said the pharmacist.

∧∧∧∧∧∧∧∧∧∧∧∧∧∧∧∧∧∧∧∧∧∧∧∧∧∧∧

What do bees like to chew?
Buzzlegum.

∧∧∧∧∧∧∧∧∧∧∧∧∧∧∧∧∧∧∧∧∧∧∧∧∧∧∧

When do ants travel fastest?
When they get on the anterstate highway.

∧∧∧∧∧∧∧∧∧∧∧∧∧∧∧∧∧∧∧∧∧∧∧∧∧∧∧

What are nature's busiest insects?
Fireflies. They're always on the glow.

∧∧∧∧∧∧∧∧∧∧∧∧∧∧∧∧∧∧∧∧∧∧∧∧∧∧∧

What kind of insects live on the moon?
Lunarticks.

Why do praying mantises have antennae?
Cable service isn't available yet in their neighborhood.

∧∧∧∧∧∧∧∧∧∧∧∧∧∧∧∧∧∧∧∧∧∧∧∧∧∧∧∧∧∧

How do snails get across oceans?
In snailboats.

∧∧∧∧∧∧∧∧∧∧∧∧∧∧∧∧∧∧∧∧∧∧∧∧∧∧∧∧∧∧

What kind of insect marries a ladybug?
a gentlemanbug.

∧∧∧∧∧∧∧∧∧∧∧∧∧∧∧∧∧∧∧∧∧∧∧∧∧∧∧∧∧∧

Stephanie: "Did you know I used to own a flea circus?"
Webster: "No. What happened to it?"
Stephanie: "A stray dog came along one day and stole the show."

∧∧∧∧∧∧∧∧∧∧∧∧∧∧∧∧∧∧∧∧∧∧∧∧∧∧∧∧∧∧

What do you call an elderly ant?
an ant-ique.

What's the difference between a bee and a fly?
You can't zip a bee.

^^^^^^^^^^^^^^^^^^^^^^^^^^^^^^^^^

Where do spiders turn when they need to know how to spell a word?
To Web-ster's Dictionary.

TONGUE TWISTER

The literary literally loaned
Larry liberal literal literature.

KNOCK-KNOCK

Knock-knock.
Who's there?
Eddie.
Eddie Who?
Eddiebody who comes too close to me might catch my cold.

^^^^^^^^^^^^^^^^^^^^^^^^^^^^^^^

Knock-knock.
Who's there?
Maybe.
Maybe Who?
Maybe-bee gun is empty. Please sell may some more bee-bees.

Knock-knock.
Who's there?
Shorty.
Shorty Who?
Shorty Simmons, who can't reach the doorbell.

^^^^^^^^^^^^^^^^^^^^^^^^^^^^^^^

Knock-knock.
Who's there?
Pasture.
Pasture Who?
Pasture bedtime. Go to sleep.

^^^^^^^^^^^^^^^^^^^^^^^^^^^^^^^

Knock-knock.
Who's there?
Annie.
Annie Who?
Annie time you're ready, come out and play. We're waiting on you.

Knock-knock.
  Who's there?
Europe.
  Europe Who?
Europe mighty early this morning.

∧∧∧∧∧∧∧∧∧∧∧∧∧∧∧∧∧∧∧∧∧∧∧∧∧∧∧

Knock-knock.
  Who's there?
Atch.
  atch who?
Sorry you have a cold.

MONEY & RICHES

Mark Twain once said money is twice-tainted. "T'ain't yours, t'ain't mine."

^^^^^^^^^^^^^^^^^^^^^^^^^^^^^^

Bob: "I know a place where we're sure to find lots of diamonds!"
Rob: "Let's go! Where is it?"
Bob: "In a deck of cards."

^^^^^^^^^^^^^^^^^^^^^^^^^^^^^^

When is a library card like a credit card?
When you use it to travel around the world.

Father: "You shouldn't waste so much money on junk toys. Don't you realize money doesn't grow on trees?"

Daughter: "Sure it does, Daddy. We always use the local bank branch, remember?"

∧∧∧∧∧∧∧∧∧∧∧∧∧∧∧∧∧∧∧∧∧∧∧∧∧∧∧∧

"I know how we can save hundreds of dollars a year on long-distance phone calls," Candie told her dad.

"Wonderful," he said. "What's your plan?"

"We can call people when they're not home!"

∧∧∧∧∧∧∧∧∧∧∧∧∧∧∧∧∧∧∧∧∧∧∧∧∧∧∧∧

Shelby: "My dad just threw away a fifty-dollar bill."

Wyatt: "What on earth did he do that for?"

Shelby: "It was a bill sent by a credit card company to the wrong address."

MUSIC

"Which musicians are usually the meanest?" Danielle asked.

"It's a toss-up," guessed Ellen, "between the ones who beat the drums and the ones who pick on the guitars."

∧∧∧∧∧∧∧∧∧∧∧∧∧∧∧∧∧∧∧∧∧∧∧∧∧∧∧∧∧∧

Which composer is squirrels' all-time favorite?
Tchaikovsky. He wrote "The Nutcracker."

∧∧∧∧∧∧∧∧∧∧∧∧∧∧∧∧∧∧∧∧∧∧∧∧∧∧∧∧∧∧

What kind of snake has red and yellow bands, is highly dangerous, and sings tenor?
A choral snake.

"How was the symphony concert?"

"It was wonderful! The orchestra played Vivaldi."

"Who won?"

∧∧∧∧∧∧∧∧∧∧∧∧∧∧∧∧∧∧∧∧∧∧∧∧∧∧∧∧∧∧

"Can you carry a tune at all?" the grumpy talent agent asked the final try-out after a long day of auditions.

"I'll let you judge that for yourself." The auditioner confidently launched into a terrible, loud rendition of a well-known popular song.

"Well, what do you think? Can I carry a tune."

"Yes," said the agent. "Please carry it out and close the door behind you."

∧∧∧∧∧∧∧∧∧∧∧∧∧∧∧∧∧∧∧∧∧∧∧∧∧∧∧∧∧∧

What do a piano and a newspaper reporter
   have in common?
They both make notes.

"May I have the pleasure of the next dance?" Mr. Mozart asked Mrs. Mozart.

"Wait just one minuet," said Mrs. Mozart.

^^^^^^^^^^^^^^^^^^^^^^^^^^^^^^^^

"Mark, I just found your guitar outside in the garbage can!" his mother said.

"I know. I put it there."

"That was your birthday present! You waited months to get it."

"Yeah, but it's no good. There's a big round hole in the middle of the sound box."

NAMES

Shelby: "Aren't you glad your mom and dad named you Lou?"
Lou: "Well, yes—but why do you ask?"
Shelby: "Because that's what all your friends call you."

∧∧∧∧∧∧∧∧∧∧∧∧∧∧∧∧∧∧∧∧∧∧∧∧∧∧∧∧∧∧

What was the name of the hunter who tangled with the bear?
Claude.

∧∧∧∧∧∧∧∧∧∧∧∧∧∧∧∧∧∧∧∧∧∧∧∧∧∧∧∧∧∧

What famous woman lives in New Orleans?
Louise E. Anna.

THE OCEAN

What happens when you tell the ocean good-bye?
It waves to you.

^^^^^^^^^^^^^^^^^^^^^^^^^^^^^^

How do they harvest the ocean floor?
With a subtractor.

^^^^^^^^^^^^^^^^^^^^^^^^^^^^^^

What's a sailor's favorite deli item?
A submarine sandwich.

^^^^^^^^^^^^^^^^^^^^^^^^^^^^^^

What keeps the ocean from going dry?
Water.

Who was the greatest chef in the British navy?
Captain Cook.

ᴧᴧᴧᴧᴧᴧᴧᴧᴧᴧᴧᴧᴧᴧᴧᴧᴧᴧᴧᴧᴧᴧᴧᴧᴧᴧᴧ

What ocean animal is the most difficult to get along with?
The crab.

ᴧᴧᴧᴧᴧᴧᴧᴧᴧᴧᴧᴧᴧᴧᴧᴧᴧᴧᴧᴧᴧᴧᴧᴧᴧᴧᴧ

Who cleans house for fish and other sea creatures?
Mermaids.

ᴧᴧᴧᴧᴧᴧᴧᴧᴧᴧᴧᴧᴧᴧᴧᴧᴧᴧᴧᴧᴧᴧᴧᴧᴧᴧᴧ

Does an octopus go around all day shaking its legs or waving its arms?

ᴧᴧᴧᴧᴧᴧᴧᴧᴧᴧᴧᴧᴧᴧᴧᴧᴧᴧᴧᴧᴧᴧᴧᴧᴧᴧᴧ

What ocean always gets things absolutely right?
The Specific Ocean.

ODDS 'N' ENDS

What has four legs, seven drawers, and flies?
Superdesk!

^^^^^^^^^^^^^^^^^^^^^^^^^^^^^^

"I can predict the future," said Carrie.
   "Sure," said Barrie. "Tell me anything at all that'll happen after today."
   "Tomorrow!" predicted Carrie.

^^^^^^^^^^^^^^^^^^^^^^^^^^^^^^

"Did you tell Stan the new airplane joke?"
   "Yeah, but I think it went right over his head."

^^^^^^^^^^^^^^^^^^^^^^^^^^^^^^

How do mountains hear?
With mountaineers.

Kristin pulled and pulled, but couldn't get the library door open.

"What's the matter?" asked a woman, approaching.

"This door must be stuck," Kristin said. "I can't pull it open."

"Can you read?" asked the woman.

"Of course I can read!" snapped Kristin.

"Then tell me what this says." The woman pointed to a word printed above the door handle. It was spelled: PUSH.

∧∧∧∧∧∧∧∧∧∧∧∧∧∧∧∧∧∧∧∧∧∧∧∧∧∧∧

"Dad, what is cargo?"

"It's a large volume of products being moved from one place to another, usually by ship or train."

"Then why isn't it called shipgo or traingo?"

∧∧∧∧∧∧∧∧∧∧∧∧∧∧∧∧∧∧∧∧∧∧∧∧∧∧∧

What did the big firecracker say to the
  little firecracker?
My pop is bigger than your pop.

Mother: "Wesley, you've gotten yourself all muddy again. You just don't have much respect for your clothes and shoes, do you?"

Wesley: "I like clothes just fine, Mom. But I certainly don't think much of shoes."

Mother: "Why not?"

Wesley: "Because most of them are either loafers or sneakers."

^^^^^^^^^^^^^^^^^^^^^^^^^^^^

A woman stopped her car beside a child who was walking home from school. "I'm new in the neighborhood," the woman explained. "How do you get to the post office from here?"

"I ride my bicycle," answered the child.

^^^^^^^^^^^^^^^^^^^^^^^^^^^^

Why was the poet unable to earn a decent living?

Because rhyme does not pay.

"You're afraid to fight me!" teased Blimpo.

"No, I'm not!" shouted Shrimpy.

"Then why won't you do it?"

"Because my mother would get mad at me and spank me."

"How would your mother find out about it?"

"She'd see the ambulance taking you to the hospital."

∧∧∧∧∧∧∧∧∧∧∧∧∧∧∧∧∧∧∧∧∧∧∧∧∧∧∧

Penny: "Please open the door for me."
Annie: "It isn't a door. It's ajar."

∧∧∧∧∧∧∧∧∧∧∧∧∧∧∧∧∧∧∧∧∧∧∧∧∧∧∧

"I hear Isaac joined the army."

"Yes. He was assigned to the paratroopers. After about twelve weeks of rigorous training, he dropped out."

"That doesn't sound good."

"Yes, it was. He had to drop out of the airplane in order to complete the instruction."

Why did Gracie want a new fountain pen?
The old one made a lot of mistakes.

∧∧∧∧∧∧∧∧∧∧∧∧∧∧∧∧∧∧∧∧∧∧∧∧∧∧∧∧∧∧

Why did the Pilgrims begin the tradition of carving turkeys on Thanksgiving?
Because rabbits were too difficult to carve.

∧∧∧∧∧∧∧∧∧∧∧∧∧∧∧∧∧∧∧∧∧∧∧∧∧∧∧∧∧∧

A group of workers were building a structure above a deep old well when one of the workers lost his balance and fell into the hole. Down, down, down he went, out of sight.

Rescue workers were summoned. They prepared ropes and lanterns, and one of them was about to descend into the dark well. "Is this well empty?" he asked the property owner.

"It was empty until today," the owner said.

"I've discovered a foolproof cure for dandruff!"

"What is it?"

"Baldness."

∧∧∧∧∧∧∧∧∧∧∧∧∧∧∧∧∧∧∧∧∧∧∧∧∧∧∧∧

Why did the apple fall from the apple tree?

Because it was ripe.

Why did the woodpecker fall from the apple tree?

Because its beak was stuck in the apple.

Why did the squirrel fall from the apple tree?

Because its tail was stapled to the woodpecker.

Why did the little boy fall from the apple tree?

He succumbed to peer pressure.

∧∧∧∧∧∧∧∧∧∧∧∧∧∧∧∧∧∧∧∧∧∧∧∧∧∧∧∧

Where does the Air Force store its bombs?
In Bombay.

"Charlie just got out of the hospital," said Marge.

"What was wrong with him?" asked Paul.

"He crashed his helicopter."

"How'd he do that?"

"He felt cold, so he turned the fan off."

^^^^^^^^^^^^^^^^^^^^^^^^^^^^^

Neighbor Gorton had a reputation for being an unpleasant old man. One day he spied a child in the branches of his largest apple tree, eating a ripe apple.

"Hey, what are you doing up there?" he demanded.

"I'm obeying your sign."

"What sign?"

"The sign that says KEEP OFF THE GRASS."

^^^^^^^^^^^^^^^^^^^^^^^^^^^^^

Where does a tailor buy his clothes?
Nowhere. He suits himself.

"Did you have a good time ice skating?"
Cybil's mother asked.

"Yes—until they closed the skating rink," Cybil said.

"Why did they close?"

"Well, it was Marvin's first time on skates. When he stumbled into the middle of the rink, he was so funny the ice cracked up."

∧∧∧∧∧∧∧∧∧∧∧∧∧∧∧∧∧∧∧∧∧∧∧∧∧∧∧∧

What are book covers for?
To help books get a good night's sleep.

∧∧∧∧∧∧∧∧∧∧∧∧∧∧∧∧∧∧∧∧∧∧∧∧∧∧∧∧

What happens if you put too many stamps on a letter?
It goes too far.

∧∧∧∧∧∧∧∧∧∧∧∧∧∧∧∧∧∧∧∧∧∧∧∧∧∧∧∧

What comes after *o*?
Boy.

Two teenagers from a foreign country were visiting America one summer. They'd never been to a movie theater and weren't sure what to do when they arrived outside.

"You buy your tickets there at the window," explained a helpful passerby. "Then you give the tickets to the usher standing at the entrance."

The visitors dutifully bought two tickets, then walked to the entrance and handed them to the usher. The usher routinely tore them in half.

The visitors looked at each other.

"What do we do now?" asked one.

"I guess we buy two more tickets," said the other with a shrug.

∧∧∧∧∧∧∧∧∧∧∧∧∧∧∧∧∧∧∧∧∧∧∧∧∧∧∧∧∧

"What should we wear to the tea party?" asked Phyllis.

"I think we should wear our nicest tea-shirts," replied Ginger.

Two hunters went to the Rocky Mountains to hunt mountain lions. They stopped at a trading post before entering the wilderness.

"Where can we find a good hunting guide?" they asked the trader and his customers.

"I'm the best guide around," volunteered a grizzled old trapper.

"Hogwash!" scoffed another. "You couldn't follow a railroad track."

∧∧∧∧∧∧∧∧∧∧∧∧∧∧∧∧∧∧∧∧∧∧∧∧∧∧∧∧∧

Why did the dieting man stand on the sidewalk all day long?
In an attempt to curb his appetite.

∧∧∧∧∧∧∧∧∧∧∧∧∧∧∧∧∧∧∧∧∧∧∧∧∧∧∧∧∧

"I'd like to buy a winter coat."
"How long do you need the sleeves?"
"About five months, November to March."

"Dad, I've decided I want to be an echo when I grow up."

"Why do you say that?"

"If I'm an echo, I'll be able to speak every language on the planet!"

^^^^^^^^^^^^^^^^^^^^^^^^^^^^^^

A family bought a nice lake cabin and settled in for their first weekend of peace and quiet, surrounded by the beauty of nature. Imagine their dismay to discover the faucets didn't work!

The father phoned the previous owner. "You told us there was running water!" he shouted.

"There is. Wait for the first rain, then look at the ceiling. You'll see."

^^^^^^^^^^^^^^^^^^^^^^^^^^^^^^

"Randall broke his leg in two places!"

"What places were they? We'd better avoid them!"

"Don't you dare go in the dining room with dirty feet!" Mom shouted. "I've just cleaned the carpet."

"But Mom, my feet are perfectly clean. That dirt you see is on my shoes."

Who steals from the rich, gives to the poor, and carries a picnic basket?
Little Red Robin Hood.

What did one nose say to the other nose?
"I smell something funny. Do you?"

What's the difference between getting splattered by a water balloon and getting smeared by an egg?
It's the difference between getting soaked and getting yoked.

Why do ceiling fans go around horizontally?
Otherwise, they would be windmills.

^^^^^^^^^^^^^^^^^^^^^^^^^^^^^^^^^^

Len: "What flying creature frequents school-rooms?"
Ben: "Spelling bees?"
Len: "No. Alpha-bats."

^^^^^^^^^^^^^^^^^^^^^^^^^^^^^^^^^^

What can run on the floor even though it doesn't have any legs?
Water.

PETS

"I love my pets," said Natasha. "It takes me five minutes just to say good-bye to them each morning before I come to school."

"What kind of pets do you have?" asked Mike.

"Three kittens, a hamster, and two dogs."

"Well, I certainly understand. It takes me more than an hour to say good-bye to my pets every morning."

"What kind of pets do you have?"

"I have fourteen goldfish and an ant farm."

A woman brought a strange-looking animal to a veterinarian's clinic. The vet did a double-take and asked, "What in the world *is* that thing?"

"It's a mattababy," the woman said.

"What's a mattababy?"

"That's what I want you to tell me."

^^^^^^^^^^^^^^^^^^^^^^^^^^^^^^^^^^

A salesman entered a yard and saw two little girls playing with a dog.

"Does your dog bite?" he asked the children.

"Oh, no, sir. Our dog has never bitten anyone."

The salesman then walked up the steps to ring the doorbell for the parents. Suddenly, the dog jumped on the porch and bit him fiercely on the leg.

"Hey, you said your dog doesn't bite!" the salesman yelled at the girls.

"Our dog doesn't. That's somebody else's dog."

The science class had show-and-tell day with pets as the theme. Mick brought in his iguana. All the children *oohed* and *ahhed* over the creature's primitive scariness.

"Why do you keep an iguana for a pet?" the teacher asked curiously.

"Because it frightens my sister," Mick replied.

∧∧∧∧∧∧∧∧∧∧∧∧∧∧∧∧∧∧∧∧∧∧∧∧∧∧∧∧∧

While walking his dog through the park, a man was startled by a kitten darting across the path.

"Whups, sorry!" called the kitten over its shoulder as it vanished into the shrubbery. "Please excuse me!"

The man stopped and stared, dropping his jaw. "I never knew a kitten that talked," he mumbled.

"Me, either," said the dog.

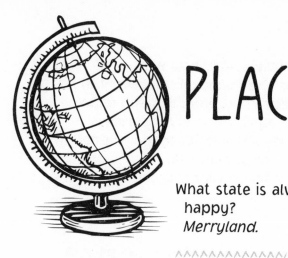

PLACES

What state is always
  happy?
Merryland.

Teacher: "Jeremy, where can we find the
  Red Sea?"
Jeremy: "Well, there's one at the top of my
  last test paper."

What state can tell the most jokes?
Jokelahoma.

Where do we find the Great Plains?
At the classic air museum.

"Western Canada is a fascinating place," said the teacher. "Did you know that some of the rocks you find there were deposited by glaciers?"

"But I don't see any glaciers in these pictures," said one student.

"They've gone to get more rocks," said a classmate slyly.

TONGUE TWISTER

Never freeze three breezy cheeses when sneezing.

PLANTS

What distinguishes a dogwood tree from all other trees?
Its bark.

^^^^^^^^^^^^^^^^^^^^^^^^^^^^^^^^^^

What kind of plants do frogs enjoy most?
Croakuses.

^^^^^^^^^^^^^^^^^^^^^^^^^^^^^^^^^^

"My grandpa likes to gather wild herbs," Myron said.
"He must be an old-thymer," laughed Biff.

"Our mathematics teacher brought a potted plant to school and put it on her desk last week," Angie told her mother. "Today, the most amazing thing happened!"

"What was it?"

"The plant grew square roots!"

∧∧∧∧∧∧∧∧∧∧∧∧∧∧∧∧∧∧∧∧∧∧∧∧∧∧

What's a tree's favorite drink?
Root beer.

∧∧∧∧∧∧∧∧∧∧∧∧∧∧∧∧∧∧∧∧∧∧∧∧∧∧

What did the tree say to the leaf at the end of summer?
Hope you have a great fall!

∧∧∧∧∧∧∧∧∧∧∧∧∧∧∧∧∧∧∧∧∧∧∧∧∧∧

What are the hottest flowers in all creation?
Sunflowers.

∧∧∧∧∧∧∧∧∧∧∧∧∧∧∧∧∧∧∧∧∧∧∧∧∧∧

What's the tallest flower in the world?
The giraffodil.

RESTAURANTS

"Pretty short menu," said Resa, trying to decide what to order for lunch. "It's printed only on one side."

"Yeah, the other side must be for customers who are full when they arrive," said Lisa.

\\^^^^^^^^^^^^^^^^^^

"I don't see spaghetti and meat sauce on this menu," complained the child.

"That's because we clean our menus after each use," said the waiter.

Brenda: "I had a dinner date at a very nice restaurant last night."
Andrea: "Who was your date?"
Brenda: "Thomas Jefferson."
Andrea: "Yeah, sure. Jefferson's been dead almost two hundred years."
Brenda: "Hmmm. Now that you mention it, he didn't say much. . . ."

ΛΛΛΛΛΛΛΛΛΛΛΛΛΛΛΛΛΛΛΛΛΛΛΛΛΛΛ

"Waitress, there's a fly in my soup!"
"Don't worry, sir. Nothing has ever been known to live very long in our soup."

ΛΛΛΛΛΛΛΛΛΛΛΛΛΛΛΛΛΛΛΛΛΛΛΛΛΛΛ

"I have a complaint," said the diner. "Bring me your head waiter."
"He's not here," said the waiter.
"Why not? Where is he?"
"He went down the street to have a burger and some fries before the dinner crowd arrives."

Diner: "What are your breakfast specials?"
Waitress: "Today we're offering hippopotamus eggs and elephant eggs."
Diner: "Give me the hippo eggs. I'm tired of
elephant yokes."

^^^^^^^^^^^^^^^^^^^^^^^^^^^^^^^^

"I'm so hungry, I could eat an elephant,"
said a customer as he sat down at a booth in
the diner.
"Coming right up," said the waitress.

^^^^^^^^^^^^^^^^^^^^^^^^^^^^^^^^

A new waitress was extremely nervous during her first evening on the job. One customer was shocked when the waitress
approached his table, clutching his rack of
lamb in both hands.
"Please take your hands off my food!" the
diner shouted.
"Oh, no, sir. I've already dropped it once. I
can't risk doing that again."

Why did the waitress lose her job?
She refused to take orders from anyone.

∧∧∧∧∧∧∧∧∧∧∧∧∧∧∧∧∧∧∧∧∧∧∧∧∧∧∧

Diner to waiter: "This chicken is so tough, I'll bet Colonel Sanders killed it when he was only a buck private."

∧∧∧∧∧∧∧∧∧∧∧∧∧∧∧∧∧∧∧∧∧∧∧∧∧∧∧

"This bread tastes funny," complained the diner.

"But you're not laughing," commented the waiter.

∧∧∧∧∧∧∧∧∧∧∧∧∧∧∧∧∧∧∧∧∧∧∧∧∧∧∧

"Do you want your coffee black?" asked the waitress.

"I didn't know coffee beans grew in any other color," said the customer.

RIDDLES

What has twenty-four eyes, two tongues, two toes, and smells terrible?
A pair of used sneakers.

^^^^^^^^^^^^^^^^^^^^^^^^^^^^^^

Where can you always get satisfaction?
From the satis-factory.

^^^^^^^^^^^^^^^^^^^^^^^^^^^^^^

What do lawyers wear?
Lawsuits.

^^^^^^^^^^^^^^^^^^^^^^^^^^^^^^

What kind of language do billboards use?
Sign language.

How long should a person's legs be?
Long enough to reach the ground.

^^^^^^^^^^^^^^^^^^^^^^^^^^^^^^^^

What has two norths, two souths, one west—
  but no east?
The fifty states of the Union.

^^^^^^^^^^^^^^^^^^^^^^^^^^^^^^^^

What kind of fruit can you pick from a
  calendar?
Dates.

^^^^^^^^^^^^^^^^^^^^^^^^^^^^^^^^

What do you call a cat who works for Xerox
  Corporation?
A copycat.

^^^^^^^^^^^^^^^^^^^^^^^^^^^^^^^^

Do magnets get married?
*No—which is remarkable, because they're all
  attractive.*

Which letter of the alphabet is an island?
T—you find it in the middle of "water."

∧∧∧∧∧∧∧∧∧∧∧∧∧∧∧∧∧∧∧∧∧∧∧∧∧∧∧∧∧

What has lots of teeth but never needs to
see a dentist?
A comb.

∧∧∧∧∧∧∧∧∧∧∧∧∧∧∧∧∧∧∧∧∧∧∧∧∧∧∧∧∧

What kind of worker gets paid to drive off
her paying customers?
The taxi driver.

∧∧∧∧∧∧∧∧∧∧∧∧∧∧∧∧∧∧∧∧∧∧∧∧∧∧∧∧∧

What kind of shoes are made with no leather?
Horseshoes.

∧∧∧∧∧∧∧∧∧∧∧∧∧∧∧∧∧∧∧∧∧∧∧∧∧∧∧∧∧

What can travel around the world while
spending its life in a corner?
A postage stamp.

Why is the river always sleepy?
Because it has rocks in its bed.

∧∧∧∧∧∧∧∧∧∧∧∧∧∧∧∧∧∧∧∧∧∧∧∧∧∧

What is it that you can touch with your left
foot but not your right foot?
Your right knee.

∧∧∧∧∧∧∧∧∧∧∧∧∧∧∧∧∧∧∧∧∧∧∧∧∧∧

What's red, has a green stem, and stays in
its room most of the day?
A tomato that's been placed on probation.

∧∧∧∧∧∧∧∧∧∧∧∧∧∧∧∧∧∧∧∧∧∧∧∧∧∧

What kind of parties do you have in the
basement?
Cellarbrations.

∧∧∧∧∧∧∧∧∧∧∧∧∧∧∧∧∧∧∧∧∧∧∧∧∧∧

What do a vacuum cleaner and a bookshelf
have in common?
They collect dust.

What's black and white and red all over?
A zebra with chickenpox.

^^^^^^^^^^^^^^^^^^^^^^^^^^^^^

What wears shoes but doesn't have feet?
A sidewalk.

^^^^^^^^^^^^^^^^^^^^^^^^^^^^^

What kind of notebook grows near trees?
Loose leaf.

^^^^^^^^^^^^^^^^^^^^^^^^^^^^^

What kind of tea can lighten up your home?
Electrici-tea.

^^^^^^^^^^^^^^^^^^^^^^^^^^^^^

What type of can contains tons of water?
A canal.

^^^^^^^^^^^^^^^^^^^^^^^^^^^^^

Who invented Kentucky-fried shoes?
Colonel Sandals.

What two words contain more than a thousand letters?
Post office.

∧∧∧∧∧∧∧∧∧∧∧∧∧∧∧∧∧∧∧∧∧∧∧∧∧

What's colorful, soft, has wings, and is an expert in arithmetic?
A mothematician.

∧∧∧∧∧∧∧∧∧∧∧∧∧∧∧∧∧∧∧∧∧∧∧∧∧

Why do police officers need to be so strong?
So they can hold up traffic.

∧∧∧∧∧∧∧∧∧∧∧∧∧∧∧∧∧∧∧∧∧∧∧∧∧

What are telephone calls in Persia?
Persian-to-Persian calls.

∧∧∧∧∧∧∧∧∧∧∧∧∧∧∧∧∧∧∧∧∧∧∧∧∧

What kind of people often climb down from trees even though they never climbed up them?
Skydivers.

What's cold and white and softly rises?
A snowflake without a clue.

∧∧∧∧∧∧∧∧∧∧∧∧∧∧∧∧∧∧∧∧∧∧∧∧∧∧∧∧

Why do firemen wear red suspenders?
To hold their pants up.

∧∧∧∧∧∧∧∧∧∧∧∧∧∧∧∧∧∧∧∧∧∧∧∧∧∧∧∧

What gets lost every time you stand up?
Your lap.

∧∧∧∧∧∧∧∧∧∧∧∧∧∧∧∧∧∧∧∧∧∧∧∧∧∧∧∧

Who makes up horror stories?
Ghost writers.

SCHOOL

"Vocabulary test tomorrow, rain or shine," reminded the teacher as the class was dismissed.

"What if it snows?" asked Will, hopefully.

^^^^^^^^^^^^^^^^^^^^^^^^^^^^^^

"How many letters are in the alphabet?" the teacher asked.

"Twenty-one," said Edward.

"No! You know there are twenty-six."

"Not right now. The D.A. and the F.B.I. are in federal court."

Teacher: "Resa, name five animals you might find in Africa."

Resa: "A lion, an elephant. . .and three zebras."

∧∧∧∧∧∧∧∧∧∧∧∧∧∧∧∧∧∧∧∧∧∧∧∧∧∧∧∧∧

"Trina, you seem to be having a lot of trouble with your spelling assignments," the teacher said.

"Yes. I guess words intimidate me."

"But they're only words! Words can't hurt you."

"I suppose not—unless you get hit by a dictionary."

∧∧∧∧∧∧∧∧∧∧∧∧∧∧∧∧∧∧∧∧∧∧∧∧∧∧∧∧∧

"Gayle, your handwriting is terrible," her father said.

"Yes, I know. I scribble deliberately."

"Why don't you want to write clearly?"

"This way, it's harder for the teacher to catch all my misspellings."

"What did you score on those two exams today?" Gina's mother asked as Gina wearily flung her backpack on the dining table.

"A hundred," Gina replied.

"That's wonderful! You've never made an A in history before!"

"Well, actually, I scored fifty in history and fifty in math."

^^^^^^^^^^^^^^^^^^^^^^^^^^^^^^^

Linda: "The teacher caught Winkie cheating on his reading test."

Rob: "Winkie knows cheating is dishonest. That was silly."

Linda: "Yeah—and even worse than you think."

Rob: "What do you mean?"

Linda: "The way the teacher knew he had cheated was his answer to the fourth question. The student sitting in front of him wrote, 'I don't know the answer.' Winkie wrote, 'I don't know the answer, either.'"

"Mindy, why are your grades so low on this report card?" Mother asked.

"Oh, it's that time of year," Mindy said. "You know everything is marked down after the holiday season."

∧∧∧∧∧∧∧∧∧∧∧∧∧∧∧∧∧∧∧∧∧∧∧∧∧∧∧∧

Teacher: "Can you name something that's harder than a diamond?"
Student: "Yes—paying for one."

∧∧∧∧∧∧∧∧∧∧∧∧∧∧∧∧∧∧∧∧∧∧∧∧∧∧∧∧

Two children met for the first time while walking home at the end of the first day of school.

"What's your name?" asked one.

"Jim White. What's yours?"

"Pete."

"Got a last name?"

"Well, I used to think my name was Pete Jenkins. But after today, I think it's Pete Be-quiet."

"I have good news and bad news," said the teacher. "The good news is that we're having only half a day of school this morning."

The class went wild with joy until the teacher quieted them.

"The bad news," he said, "is that we'll have the other half this afternoon."

∧∧∧∧∧∧∧∧∧∧∧∧∧∧∧∧∧∧∧∧∧∧∧∧∧∧∧∧∧

"Where do we get pineapples?" asked the teacher.

"From pine trees," guessed the student.

∧∧∧∧∧∧∧∧∧∧∧∧∧∧∧∧∧∧∧∧∧∧∧∧∧∧∧∧∧

Teacher: "Shirley, compose a sentence that begins with 'I.'"
Shirley: "I is—"
Teacher: "Never say, 'I is.' It's 'He is' or 'She is,' but 'I am.' Begin your sentence, 'I am. . . .'"
Shirley: "I am the ninth letter of the alphabet."

"Did you play hooky from school yesterday to go fishing?" the teacher asked.

"No, sir," said Dennis. "I played hooky to go to the carnival."

^^^^^^^^^^^^^^^^^^^^^^^^^^^^^^^^^^

"I didn't see you in any of our classes yesterday," said Kimberly. "You must've missed school."

"Not much," said Kenneth.

^^^^^^^^^^^^^^^^^^^^^^^^^^^^^^^^^^

"What is a synonym?" the English teacher asked.

"It's one of the words I use when I can't spell the main word," the honest student replied.

^^^^^^^^^^^^^^^^^^^^^^^^^^^^^^^^^^

Teacher: "Who's the Speaker of the House?"
Student: "Daddy."

"Did you learn anything at school today?" Jeff's dad asked.

"I guess not," Jeff said. "They're making us return tomorrow."

^^^^^^^^^^^^^^^^^^^^^^^^^^^^^

Why was Mrs. Johnson's class abuzz?
It was having a spelling bee.

^^^^^^^^^^^^^^^^^^^^^^^^^^^^^

Mother was reading in the den when Beth came to the door. "Mom, do you think you could sign your name in the dark?"

"I've never tried, dear, but I probably could."

"Good!" said Beth, switching off the light. "I need for you to sign my report card."

^^^^^^^^^^^^^^^^^^^^^^^^^^^^^

Teacher: "Jamie, how do you spell 'canoe'?"
Jamie: "K-n-e-w."

A rule was posted in large letters in the school hallway: SHOES REQUIRED IN THE CAFETERIA.

In the margin, someone had scribbled: SOCKS MUST GO TO THE GYM.

∧∧∧∧∧∧∧∧∧∧∧∧∧∧∧∧∧∧∧∧∧∧∧∧∧∧∧∧∧∧

Mother was eager to hear about Brenda's first day at school. "So how do you think you're doing so far?"

"Well, apparently, I'm one of the advanced students," Brenda remarked.

"Oh, really? What makes you think that?"

"They put me at the head of a row."

SCIENCE

What kind of chewing gum do scientists prefer?
Experiment Gum.

"Do you know why lightning rarely strikes the same place twice?" asked the science teacher.

"Because after lightning strikes it the first time," a bright student responded, "the same place is *gone!*"

Teacher: "Who was the first person to circle the earth in space?"
Student: "The man in the moon."

"What would happen if there was no such thing as gravity?" the teacher asked.

"We could all fly!" came the answer.

^^^^^^^^^^^^^^^^^^^^^^^^^^^^^

"The spaceships of the next century will travel faster than the speed of light!" the science teacher marveled to her class.

"Then what kind of lights will they have inside them?" asked a student.

^^^^^^^^^^^^^^^^^^^^^^^^^^^^^

"Do you understand exactly what biology is?" the teacher asked on the first day of class.

One student raised her hand. "I think it's the science my mom practices whenever she goes to the shopping mall."

^^^^^^^^^^^^^^^^^^^^^^^^^^^^^

What do astronomers do to relax?
They enjoy reading comet books.

Science teacher: "How can herpetologists tell the age of a snake?"
Student: "Track down its birth certificate."

∧∧∧∧∧∧∧∧∧∧∧∧∧∧∧∧∧∧∧∧∧∧∧∧∧∧∧

What did the seismologist say to the earthquake?
"This is all your fault."

∧∧∧∧∧∧∧∧∧∧∧∧∧∧∧∧∧∧∧∧∧∧∧∧∧∧∧

"I think Thomas Edison must have been the most brilliant person who ever lived," said Kate.

"What makes you think so?" asked her teacher.

"He invented the lightbulb. Then, to give people a reason to keep the lights on all night, he invented the phonograph!"

∧∧∧∧∧∧∧∧∧∧∧∧∧∧∧∧∧∧∧∧∧∧∧∧∧∧∧

What was Voltaire famous for?
He invented the volt.

What kind of telephones do they use in the space shuttle?
Phones with very long cords.

∧∧∧∧∧∧∧∧∧∧∧∧∧∧∧∧∧∧∧∧∧∧∧∧∧∧∧

Why did Benjamin Franklin make the first eyeglasses?
To make a spectacle of himself.

∧∧∧∧∧∧∧∧∧∧∧∧∧∧∧∧∧∧∧∧∧∧∧∧∧∧∧

What goes up when you count down?
A rocket.

SPORTS

When is a football team
like an airplane?
When it makes a touchdown.

^^^^^^^^^^^^^^^^^^^^^^^^^^^^^

An auctioneer was persuaded to join some
friends in a round of golf. He'd never been
on a golf course before.

"Fore!" shouted one of his friends, hitting
a tee shot.

"Do I hear four and a quarter?" barked
the auctioneer without thinking.

^^^^^^^^^^^^^^^^^^^^^^^^^^^^^

What sport do mosquitoes enjoy?
Skindiving.

Two boys attended a high school basketball game.

"Boy, that big forward for the other team sure is tall!" marveled one.

"Yeah, I'll bet he needs a ladder to shave," said the other.

^^^^^^^^^^^^^^^^^^^^^^^^^^^^^^

What does a cake have in common with a baseball game?
The batter.

^^^^^^^^^^^^^^^^^^^^^^^^^^^^^^

What's purple and has twenty-two legs, four backs, and two ends?
A football team from Mars.

^^^^^^^^^^^^^^^^^^^^^^^^^^^^^^

Mother: "Did you hear that shattering noise? It sounded like a window breaking."
Son: "Didn't hear a thing, Mom. Have you seen our softball?"

A baseball pitcher was so angry he screamed at the first baseman, screamed at the shortstop, and screamed at the catcher. Finally, he took off his glove, slung it on the mound and began stomping on it, still screaming.

"What in the world does he think he's doing?" one outfielder called to another.

"He's throwing his best pitch, known as a tantrum."

∧∧∧∧∧∧∧∧∧∧∧∧∧∧∧∧∧∧∧∧∧∧∧∧∧∧∧∧∧∧

"Dad! Dad! I won the gold medal in the broad jump!"

"That's terrific! I know you're proud."

"Yeah. May I have twenty dollars?"

"What for?"

"To have it bronzed."

∧∧∧∧∧∧∧∧∧∧∧∧∧∧∧∧∧∧∧∧∧∧∧∧∧∧∧∧∧∧

What's black and white and goes 150 miles an hour?

A newspaper being read by a stockcar driver.

"Hey, I've got great news for you!" Brewster said to his buddy Val after the track and field tryouts. "I just overheard the coaches say they've selected you for the hammer throw unit."

"That's great!" Val yelled. "I'd better start practicing, huh?"

"Well, actually," said Brewster, his smile disappearing, "there's sort of a down-side to it."

"What do you mean?"

"They want you to be the catcher."

^^^^^^^^^^^^^^^^^^^^^^^^^^^^^

What does a football game have in common with a dollar?
It consists of four quarters.

^^^^^^^^^^^^^^^^^^^^^^^^^^^^^

What happens when two ropes get into a contest?
They always tie.

What do skydivers do when their parachutes don't open?
They yell for the airplane crew to lower a rope.

∧∧∧∧∧∧∧∧∧∧∧∧∧∧∧∧∧∧∧∧∧∧∧∧∧∧∧∧∧∧

Why do runners stretch their legs before beginning a race?
They know if they can make their legs longer, they'll run faster!

∧∧∧∧∧∧∧∧∧∧∧∧∧∧∧∧∧∧∧∧∧∧∧∧∧∧∧∧∧∧

Why did the basketball team flood the gymnasium?
It was the only way they could sink any baskets.

∧∧∧∧∧∧∧∧∧∧∧∧∧∧∧∧∧∧∧∧∧∧∧∧∧∧∧∧∧∧

"I keep my baseball glove in the car," said Bruce, making a detour to fetch it before joining the neighborhood ball game.

"Why do you keep it there?" asked Vernon.

"The car has a glove compartment."

Why did the golfer carry an extra shirt and pair of pants in his golf bag?
In case he got a hole in one.

∧∧∧∧∧∧∧∧∧∧∧∧∧∧∧∧∧∧∧∧∧∧∧∧∧∧∧∧

Which Olympic athletes operate moving van lines in their later years?
The boxers.

∧∧∧∧∧∧∧∧∧∧∧∧∧∧∧∧∧∧∧∧∧∧∧∧∧∧∧∧

What do baseball players on third base like to sing?
"There's no place like home."

TALL TALES

"My dad sure has big feet."
"Yeah? How big?"
"They're so big his toes start turning the corner while his heel is still a block behind."

⌄⋀⋀⋀⋀⋀⋀⋀⋀⋀⋀⋀⋀

Ryan: "My great-grandfather was a famous polar bear hunter."

Bryan: "Where?"

Ryan: "In Mississippi."

Bryan: "No way! There are no polar bears in Mississippi."

Ryan: "Nope, not since my great-grandfather finished with 'em."

"My grandfather was a ship captain," Marshall said. "You should hear him tell about the time he was transporting a cargo of yo-yos from Japan to California, and this terrible storm came up!"

"What happened?" asked Sid.

"The ship kept sinking to the bottom of the ocean, and then rising to the surface, and sinking again, and rising. . . ."

∧∧∧∧∧∧∧∧∧∧∧∧∧∧∧∧∧∧∧∧∧∧∧∧∧∧∧∧∧

"I swallowed a pocket watch when I was only four years old, and it's still inside my stomach," said Jacque.

"Wow!" said Jean. "That's gruesome! Does it ever give you a problem?"

"No—except that it's difficult to wind."

∧∧∧∧∧∧∧∧∧∧∧∧∧∧∧∧∧∧∧∧∧∧∧∧∧∧∧∧∧

They say Abraham Lincoln was so tall it took his head five minutes to realize his toes were frozen.

"I've figured out how to catch man-eating tigers," announced Gilbert.

"Oh, really?" his father said. "What tools would you use?"

"Binoculars, tweezers, and a paper sack," Gilbert said confidently.

"This sounds fascinating. What's your method?"

"I hide in a tree until I see a man-eating tiger coming, way off in the distance. I turn the binoculars backward and look at the tiger through the wrong end. This shrinks the tiger to the size of a fly. Then I just grab the little critter with the tweezers and whisk it into the bag."

^^^^^^^^^^^^^^^^^^^^^^^^^^^^^^^^^^

Brittany: "My great-grandfather helped build the Grand Coulee Dam."

Artie: "That's nothing. My great-grandfather helped kill the Dead Sea."

VACATION

"Ma'am, I need to buy a nonstop plane ticket to New York City, please," the Montana rancher told the airline agent.

The agent checked the flight schedule. "We can't get you to New York nonstop from here. We can get you there via Buffalo."

The rancher thought it over. "Well," he said, "I've never ridden a buffalo, but I'll give it a try."

∧∧∧∧∧∧∧∧∧∧∧∧∧∧∧∧∧∧∧∧∧∧∧∧∧∧∧∧∧∧

Where do dogs love to go on vacation?
To Jellystone Bark.

Two children played the age-old game of counting cows while riding in the backseat of their parents' car.

"I just spotted one!" shouted one child.

"Don't be ridiculous," scoffed the other. "That cow already had spots."

∧∧∧∧∧∧∧∧∧∧∧∧∧∧∧∧∧∧∧∧∧∧∧∧∧∧∧∧∧∧∧∧

"I thought you complained that it rained the whole time you were on vacation," Matt said. "So how did you get such a great suntan?"

"This is not a suntan," said Pat. "This is a rusty body."

TONGUE TWISTER

Meek Nick eats green grapes.
Bleak Mick meets Greek apes.

WEATHER

"Did you hear they've scheduled the town Christmas parade Saturday afternoon?"

"Yes. I wonder what will happen if it snows Saturday afternoon?"

"Then I guess they'll have to hold the parade Saturday morning."

^^^^^^^^^^^^^^^^^^^^^^^^^^^^^^^^^

"We sure have been getting a lot of rain," Andrew commented.

"Yeah," agreed Tonya. "I hope they've started building an ark down at the zoo."

What holds up the sun?
Sunbeams.

∧∧∧∧∧∧∧∧∧∧∧∧∧∧∧∧∧∧∧∧∧∧∧∧∧∧∧∧∧∧∧

How do people who live in the desert stay cool?
They take turns standing in one another's shadow.

"What's the difference between weather and climate?" the teacher asked.

"Weather is the abbreviation for climate," one student volunteered.

TONGUE TWISTER

Justin Judge judges justly.

Lisa laughed listlessly.

WORK & PLAY

"You children watch too much TV and sit around and do nothing all day," Father scolded. "You should come help me work in the yard."

"But it's too much trouble," protested Jessica.

"Nonsense. Work is good for you."

"Then shouldn't we save some for tomorrow?"

YOU KNOW WHAT YOU GET WHEN...?

. . .you cross a school bus with an octopus?
An octo bus.

^^^^^^^^^^^^^^^^^^^^^^^^^^^^^^^^

. . .you cross a parrot with a monkey?
A critter that can explain all the mischief it gets into.

^^^^^^^^^^^^^^^^^^^^^^^^^^^^^^^^

. . .you take a dog to a beauty parlor?
A shampoodle.

. . .you cross a hunting dog with a gold football uniform?
A golden receiver.

^^^^^^^^^^^^^^^^^^^^^^^^^^^^^^^

. . .you cross a lion with a computer?
A maneframe.

^^^^^^^^^^^^^^^^^^^^^^^^^^^^^^^

. . .you cross mathematics with seaweed?
Algae-bra.

^^^^^^^^^^^^^^^^^^^^^^^^^^^^^^^

. . .you cross a crab and a mockingbird?
A walkie-talkie.

^^^^^^^^^^^^^^^^^^^^^^^^^^^^^^^

. . .you put a rotor blade on a snail?
A shellicopter.

^^^^^^^^^^^^^^^^^^^^^^^^^^^^^^^

. . .you cross a hog with a tree?
Porky Twig.

. . .you cross an octopus with a chicken?
Lots of drumsticks.

^^^^^^^^^^^^^^^^^^^^^^^^^^^^^^

. . .you cross a mathematical genius with a
basketball star?
A fine mathlete.

^^^^^^^^^^^^^^^^^^^^^^^^^^^^^^

. . .you cross a groundhog with a basketball
net?
An extended basketball season.

^^^^^^^^^^^^^^^^^^^^^^^^^^^^^^

. . .you start across a river in a rotten boat?
No further than halfway.

^^^^^^^^^^^^^^^^^^^^^^^^^^^^^^

. . .you cross a kangaroo with a cement
truck?
Potholes across the Outback.

. . .you cross a skunk with a rattlesnake?
Something you wouldn't want to share a locker with.

∧∧∧∧∧∧∧∧∧∧∧∧∧∧∧∧∧∧∧∧∧∧∧∧∧∧∧∧∧∧

. . .you cross a church steeple with a pair of jeans?
Bellbottoms.

∧∧∧∧∧∧∧∧∧∧∧∧∧∧∧∧∧∧∧∧∧∧∧∧∧∧∧∧∧∧

. . .you assign Superman to a computer crash?
A screensaver.

∧∧∧∧∧∧∧∧∧∧∧∧∧∧∧∧∧∧∧∧∧∧∧∧∧∧∧∧∧∧

. . .you cross a church bell with a humming-bird?
A humdinger.

∧∧∧∧∧∧∧∧∧∧∧∧∧∧∧∧∧∧∧∧∧∧∧∧∧∧∧∧∧∧

. . .you cross an orange with a famous story-teller?
Mother Juice.

. . .your cat swallows a ball of yarn?
Mittens!

AAAAAAAAAAAAAAAAAAAAAAAAAAAAA

. . .you cross a concrete truck with a chicken?
a block-layer.

AAAAAAAAAAAAAAAAAAAAAAAAAAAAA

. . .you put a cow on a trampoline?
a gigantic milkshake.

AAAAAAAAAAAAAAAAAAAAAAAAAAAAA

. . .you cross an octopus with a cow?
a cow that can draw its own milk.

AAAAAAAAAAAAAAAAAAAAAAAAAAAAA

. . .you cross a cow with a chicken?
Roost beef.

AAAAAAAAAAAAAAAAAAAAAAAAAAAAA

. . .you cross a snowman with a guard dog?
Frostbite.

. . .you cross a bulldog with a computer?
Both a bark and a byte.

∧∧∧∧∧∧∧∧∧∧∧∧∧∧∧∧∧∧∧∧∧∧∧∧∧

. . .you cross a skunk with a honey-colored
bear?
Winnie the Pe-yew!

∧∧∧∧∧∧∧∧∧∧∧∧∧∧∧∧∧∧∧∧∧∧∧∧∧

. . .a reptile scientist marries a funeral home
director?
Hiss and hearse.

∧∧∧∧∧∧∧∧∧∧∧∧∧∧∧∧∧∧∧∧∧∧∧∧∧

. . .you cross a dentist with a wild animal?
A molar bear.

TONGUE TWISTER

Three blind mice blew bugles.

Floyd fed the flies fried fly food.

Sue Sleuth slowly solved the sloppy case.